I highly commend this book to you
for bringing timeless wisdom to l.. _
ways, making it practical and easy to apply.
I foresee this book will become a well-thumbed manual
for many and an essential read for emerging and
seasoned leaders alike.

Rev. Celia Apeagyei-Collins
Founder and President of The Rehoboth Foundation

An antidote to the self-help movement that tends to
emphasise personal goals for personal gain, this book
will encourage and equip you to seek out a different
path, one that leads to community transformation,
worked out in collaboration with others who share the
same passion for justice, and the same longing for
change that you carry in your own heart.

Susie Hart MBE
Founder & CEO of Artizan International
Founder of Neema Crafts Centre in Tanzania

This book is expertly crafted, richly researched, and
authentically communicated from the heart. Let Darren
put fire in your belly and bring dreams into reality.

Phil Knox
Author, Speaker, Missiology Specialist

A heartfelt yet practical guide to help you deconstruct the
norms of 'leadership' we generally acquire, and then
upgrade them, so that you and those you impact can fly
to new heights, personally, professionally and
prophetically. This is more than a book, it's a toolbox!

Seth Pinnock, Symphony
Strategic Innovator, Singer-Songwriter,
Social Entrepreneur

Darren takes us on an energetic tour around different aspects of goal-focused strategy, injecting a strong sense of 'you can do this!' to anyone driven to bring about change.

Amanda Toombs
Golddigger Trust Founder & Creative Director

Having been involved in leadership development across different sectors for three decades, I highly recommend this book to emerging leaders at all levels.

Geoff Baxter OBE
Founder, Charity CEO, Innovator

Darren Richard's book is an inspiring and practical guide to authentic leadership, using a relatable plane parable and timeless wisdom to empower emerging and seasoned leaders alike, and reminding us that our character and leadership are inseparable.

Errol Lawson
Author, Church Leader, Leadership Coach

I unreservedly recommend 'The Plane Parable', to everyone seeking personal transformation. This book springs from Darren Richards' wealth of experience in leadership over 20 years. It is well written, insightful, and empowering. I believe it will be a huge blessing to every reader.

Musa Bako
Author, Senior Pastor at Victory Assembly Sheffield

The Plane Parable is for the dreamers who dare to believe they can make a difference. We can either create change or change will create us, and in this book Darren equips his readers in how to create change and lead. Be challenged, inspired and empowered as you work through this book.

Nande Boss
Global Speaker, Author & Change Maker

If you are looking for guidance and motivation to make your dream a reality you need to read this book.

Paul Unsworth,
Kahaila Entrepreneur, Charity CEO, Leader

THE
PLANE
PARABLE

How to lift-off, lead and secede

PublishU Ltd

www.PublishU.com

Dedication

For Dad – your leadership legacy lives on.

To Caroline – your love and wisdom keep me on course.

To my boys – may you soar high, live well, and laugh loud.

Acknowledgements

Thanks be to God, the Author and Perfecter of my faith.

Love and thanks to my grandparents and to Stephen and Gill, for your prayers.

Special thanks to Rev. Celia, for believing in me.

And sincere thanks to Barry, Matt, Mum, Chris, Tracey and Joti for making this book possible.

I am forever grateful.

*"Hope deferred makes the heart sick,
but a longing fulfilled is a tree of life."*

The Bible

Proverbs chapter 13, verse 12

HEADING

HABITS　　　HEART

LEADING
YOURSELF

HEARD　　HOPE　　HELD

LEADING
OTHERS

HUMILITY　　HONESTY

LEADING
LONGEVITY

HANDOVER

Contents

*Who we are and how we lead
are irrevocably entwined.*

Foreword

Darren Richards' book takes off and starts inspiring, empowering and challenging the reader from the very first chapter; appealing to those who are still dreaming about what they want to achieve – emerging leaders and seasoned leaders alike – pushing them to more purposeful and meaningful living. It's definitely an achiever's practical handbook. The language is reader-friendly, the anecdotes relevant, and his use of the Plane Parable as an example, easy to identify with.

The greatest challenge we face in the twenty-first century is a lack of integrous, competent leadership. Our increasingly secular culture would have us believe that integrity and influence are two unconnected factors. We're asked to buy-in to a long-debunked lie, that the person we are behind closed doors will not influence our role and responsibilities as a leader. It's simply not so. And in his modern fable of a plane learning the valuable lessons of leadership, Darren shines light on the truth of the matter: *who we are* and *how we lead* are irrevocably entwined.

Those who chase their dream, must also nurture the qualities and necessary character traits that set true leaders apart. Those we lead deserve it, our outcomes are a result of it. We need moral courageous giants, able to earn buy-in from the communities they serve, in order to progress the causes they steward. People who can stand tall, enabling others to stand on their shoulders.

Johann Wolfgang von Goethe, German statesman, poet and playwright states that "There is nothing more dangerous than an active ignorance." The narrative of this book takes you on a journey through the many stages of making vision a reality. From self-belief, setting up a project and building a team, to facing tough times as a leader and raising others up. This simple story of a plane holds valuable secrets, tips and techniques that will give you an advantage in your everyday relationships as well as your leadership spheres.

In a world where change is ongoing and complex, and it no longer has a beginning nor an end, yesterday's leadership strategies won't necessarily work today. New thinking and new perspectives, grounded in proven principles, are a must.

We need an emerging generation of energetic and trustworthy leaders to take up the responsibility, win people over and model authentic leadership, in order to affect meaningful change in our hurting world. We need leaders with courage and steel, not professional skills and qualifications alone.

Take this book. Read it. Learn it. Keep returning to it. Then run – run with your vision! Others depend on it.

Hear the call to the poor, the broken, the ill-treated and the outcast. Use this handbook to get your dream airborne and then take it high into the stratosphere, where others will see you and be inspired to do likewise.

"He who beats the drum has no idea how far the sound travels." (African Proverb)

Rev. Celia Apeagyei-Collins

Founder and President of The Rehoboth Foundation
Founder of Young Emerging Leaders
Leadership Consultant
International Speaker

No one else in history has ever had your special mix of skills, talents, relationships, passions, stories and experiences.
In short, you are a masterpiece.

Chapter 1
TIME FLIES

"The most difficult thing is the decision to act;
the rest is merely tenacity."
Amelia Earhart

In 1903, the New York Times published a scathing article. It claimed a "flying machine" would be invented through "the combined and continuous efforts of mathematicians and mechanicians in ... **one million to ten million years**."

Sixty nine days later, the Wright Brothers achieved the first powered flight with their prototype plane "The Wright Flyer."

Just imagine how they felt, climbing out of their beds on Thursday, 17 December 1903. In many ways, they were Noah building an ark, day after dry, dusty day. These brothers had no idea this date would go down in history.

For them, it was just another morning, waking up to attempt the impossible. Another day trying to achieve a feat they were told would take myriads of experts, millions of years, if indeed it could be done at all.

And yet, Wilbur and Orville Wright woke up and decided to try and fly, once again, despite creeping self-doubt, fears of ridicule and the high risk of horrible injury.

Despite a series of failures, one after the other, innumerable disappointments and the world's press mocking them mercilessly, the two brothers decided to simply try again. They seemed destined to be remembered as history's biggest losers; international laughing stocks clinging to an absurd fantasy that a person could soar in the sky like Icarus.

But they didn't give up on their dream, give in to their detractors, nor give way to their fears.

After four years of trial and error, painstaking research, tinkering with pitch, power, weight and balance, and experimenting with countless materials, they finally refined the precise parameters. And so, Wilbur and Orville gave their impossible dream one more go.

It's fair to say that this choice changed the course of history.

Perhaps if they'd stumbled over the cat or read the wrong newspaper over breakfast, they might have decided to give up.

But the Wright Brothers were dreamers. They weren't deluded; they were determined.

So out they went into the cold, to try something so miraculous that it verged on magic: lifting off the ground while seated in a craft that was heavier than air.

And that's when it happened.

At 10:35am, the Wright brothers covered a hundred and twenty feet in twelve seconds, ushering in the age of powered aviation.

Orville became the first pilot of the very first engine-powered aeroplane – just ten million years earlier than billed. At that moment, a windy and treeless dune with soft sand, called Kitty Hawk, transformed into the world's first runway and airfield.

Soon this "first" flight inspired one pioneer after another. Each new dreamer blazed a trail for the next record-breaker to follow. First after first, in quick succession:

Raymonde de Laroche became the first female pilot to receive a licence, just six years after that first flight by the Wright brothers.

She was then followed by the first woman to fly solo and non-stop across the vast Atlantic Ocean – Amelia Earhart.

Then in 1912, a mere nine years after that first powered flight, Emory Conrad Malick became the first black pilot to earn a licence to fly, having constructed his own biplane.

One first after another, until the very first passenger jet sped down the runway and took flight in 1949. The British De Havilland Comet was designed by Geoffrey de Havilland. He was so inspired by The Wright brothers that he quit his job and borrowed money to pursue his own aviation dream. Having worked on technical designs for a company that built double-decker buses, De Havilland later conceived the world's first jet-powered passenger plane, for all intents and purposes: a flying bus.

These days, powered flights are not limited to earth. The first flight on another planet took place in 2012, when the *Ingenuity* helicopter flew on Mars, a century after the Wright's displayed their own ingenuity.

All of these "firsts" began with two dreamers climbing out of bed on a chilly December morning to attempt the impossible. While others were preparing for Christmas, the Wright brothers were breathing warm air on frozen fingers and adjusting fragile parts they'd cobbled together from a bicycle workshop. Out on that sandy dune, they risked their life on a dream that others thought utterly futile. Wilbur even likened it to a sickness, writing:

"For some years, I've been afflicted with the belief that flight is possible to man. My disease has increased in severity and I feel that it will soon cost me an increased amount of money, if not my life."

By the end of that historic day, The Wright Flyer could stay in the air for almost a minute, climbing close to a thousand feet up in the air. That's some serious progress, considering powered flight was only a dream when they ate their breakfast that morning.

The Wrights' incredible bravery, dogged perseverance and engineering ingenuity gave rise to a gravity-defying machine that inspired a million "firsts." When they fired up their little aeroengine, they fuelled the imaginations of pioneers, scientists, entrepreneurs, writers, engineers and heroes. This spark of belief burned in the hearts of countless dreamers down throughout the decades.

What about YOU?

You've just read a story about two dreamers and the difference that a dream can make in the lives of other people. So, my question to you is: *what is your dream?*

Do you have a seemingly impossible hope, hidden inside you? Or even just the beginnings of an idea, that just might encourage a few people where you live?

What's the dream you intend to pursue "someday" when the time is right and when you can afford it? What's the plan you'll put into action once life slows down and when you can summon the courage or, perhaps, when you figure out where to start?

We'll call this your "Someday dream": the idea you have that could make a difference to someone and the burden you carry for a community you care about.

If this "Someday dream" never happens, then someone else will miss out. It matters because you matter; you are completely unique! No one else in history has ever had your special mix of skills, talents, relationships, passions, stories and experiences. In short, you are a masterpiece: priceless and irreplaceable. You're one of a kind and you have limitless potential to make a difference in the lives of others, especially those less fortunate than you.

Only you can bring your valuable and unique contribution to the world and inspire others in the process. Put simply, there's something that you can do that others cannot. So, please don't let anything stand in your way: Skills can be learned. Confidence can be cultivated. Motivation can be mustered. Fears can be conquered. And doubts can be defeated.

So many people – too many people – daydream about doing something meaningful, making their mark and offering a contribution. Many are just waiting for the right time to step out and get going with their dream. But the real tragedy is that most people never do. They'd rather not risk trying in case they fail and make a fool of themselves. Or they wait too long, for some perfect moment someday, that never comes. Lack of money, lack of time, lack of energy or lack of knowing how, leaves most dreams unfulfilled, gathering dust on the proverbial shelf. These neglected, dusty dreams will never see the light of day. They will never change a life or inspire a "first" anything.

There are so many excuses for giving up on our dream before we even get going. Perhaps some of these sound familiar?

"...after I'm qualified."

"...when I've made more money."

"...after I've had kids."

"...when I have more time."

These excuses soon melt away, to be replaced by regrets:

"I could have been..."

"I'd hoped I would..."

"I missed it, because..."

The truth is, you'll never have more time. You'll never have enough money to overcome a fear of stepping out. And you'll never feel truly ready or qualified. In fact, you'll only ever amass more excuses as the years roll by.

It's so tragic that so many people fail to fulfil their potential when everything they need is right there at their fingertips. Most settle for "someday" and "one day," instead of seizing *this* day.

Why let your doubts grow into regrets? No one wants to sit and say one day: "I should have," "I would have," or "I could have." Instead, be a dreamer who acts. You can be the *would be, could be, should be* leader, who decided to step out and try at least.

What if you have the kernel of an idea that someone is waiting for? Whether that's your family, your friends, your local community, your country, or even the entire world, as in the case of the Wright brothers. The truth is *you can change lives.* And someone is waiting for your dream. You can be sure of that. But if you wait for "some day," your family, friends and community will miss out.

So, what's stopping you?

You can make the world a better, fairer and kinder place with your dream. And you don't have to be a billionaire or a genius inventor to do it.

For starters, you already have a head start on the Wright brothers. Consider for a moment that you are living at a time in history when you don't need a publishing company to advertise your idea, you only need a smartphone. You don't need a library or university to learn new skills, just an internet connection. And you don't have to pay thousands for a TV campaign or radio ad when you can start a podcast or share your thoughts on social media. More or less all of the knowledge, wisdom and education amassed throughout the entire span of recorded history; hundreds of generations and thousands of civilisations worth of learning and insight, are available to you free of charge. You're living through the digital revolution. That's a pretty big advantage.

Secondly, you are rich. The vast majority of people who read this book will be incredibly wealthy and privileged, in global terms. You may not feel like you're very "rich," but a quarter of the world doesn't have a toilet. So, you actually woke up in paradise this morning, from the perspective of someone living in extreme poverty.

If you can get yourself a glass of clean water to drink, if you can reach into the fridge to fix breakfast, if you slept in a warm bed in a safe home last night, then you're richer than three quarters of the world's population. In fact, since you're reading this, you probably went to school and you may well have a bank account too, which means you're actually in the top 10 per cent of the world's wealthiest people.

We all look around at our friends and family to gauge how wealthy and successful we are, but it's clear that we have so much to offer and so much to be thankful for. When you realise you have opportunities and privileges that millions of other people can only dream of, it changes your whole outlook. When there are millions of men, women, boys and girls right now, whose dream is simply to survive until tomorrow, surely, we should make the most of the rich resources and bountiful blessings that we possess? Even if your dream is not yet fully formed, there has literally, historically, never been a better time to explore it further.

After all, what do you have to lose?

Since you asked...

"A lot. I have a lot to lose," is what you're probably thinking right now. It's fine to read a book that motivates you to take a risk and help others, but it's the same old culprits that hold us back: self-doubt, self-consciousness or good old-fashioned selfish reservations. As the old adage says, "time flies when you're having fun." And when life feels reasonably comfortable as well as complex and cluttered, months and even years can pass you by before you make a start on your idea. Reading a book about achieving your "Someday dream" is easy enough, but actually doing it, amid the business and bustle of real life is another matter entirely. It's not just that we're short on time, we also know that we might fail, look foolish or lose money. On top of these reservations are other hurdles. Are any of these stumbling blocks preventing you from believing you can achieve your dream?

Comparison

It's said that "comparison is the thief of joy." It's also a plughole down which your dreams will drain. Whatever your age, skin colour and ability, please don't compare yourself to anyone else. You don't have to be the smartest or best. Just take what you have and put it to work. You'll always come up short trying to be like someone else.

Age

If you're young, you can enjoy reach, know-how and credibility even multinational companies can't buy. Don't let anyone disqualify you because of your age. If you're older, you have life experience and wisdom to draw on. Age is just a number, not a barrier.

Difficulty

It won't be easy. Dreams have never been easy. If someone tells you it will be easy, then check to see how much money they're asking for – that should be a clue. Dreams are hard graft. But dreams are worth it. Our brains are hardwired for safety, comfort and conformity – not for standing out, suffering or going it alone. Pursuing a dream goes against our most primal drives for an easy life and our "stay with the herd" survival instinct. Recognise that you'd rather sit and surf fun videos or just stay in bed. Then, decide to disregard those impulses and do something you'll be proud of for the rest of your life.

Perfection

The perfect coffee. The perfect holiday. The perfect speech. None of these things exist. Different things are perfect on different days, for different people. What makes something perfect depends on the season or situation. Different leaders are needed for different causes and projects. So, what's perfect for you in your situation won't be perfect for another leader in theirs. You'll never feel you've had enough sleep, training or experience to create the perfect anything. Set aside your unrealistic standards and settle for "good enough." That may sound reckless, but it's a whole lot more fruitful than not doing anything at all because you're waiting for absolute perfection. It's never going to be perfect and that's okay. Perfectionists seldom change the world. Dreamers and do-ers change the world.

Originality

Your dream doesn't have to be completely original or unique. The fact that you're doing it, makes it unique and original. Just because you've seen it done before, doesn't necessarily mean you shouldn't do it too, in your own way. True creativity is about taking what's been done before and adding to it or making it relevant to a new audience. As Aristotle once said: "It's not once, nor twice, but times without number that the same ideas make their appearance in the world."

As an aside, you'll notice Aristotle, the Greek "father of rhetoric," is quoted a few times in this book. Although far from perfect as a man, as a philosopher Aristotle understood that habits and moral character are crucial. He also knew how to win others to a cause, and so turn vision into reality. You'll often see Aristotle's wisdom repackaged in popular culture, but here you'll find the original quotes.

The plane made plain...

This book begins with a simple story: The Plane Parable. It's a modern fable about a reluctant passenger jet. Its purpose is simply to make the key points more memorable. After the parable, subsequent chapters unpack the meaning of this allegory.

The book is also divided into three main sections, mirroring the three ways a plane can move in the air: Pitch, Roll and Yaw.

PITCH – where the nose of the plane moves up to climb or down to descend. This first section is about self-management, or **how to lead yourself**.

ROLL – where a plane's wings dip down on one side and raise up on the other side. This middle section is about **leading other people**; addressing their concerns, questions and even opposition.

YAW – where the plane's rudder pivots to turn the plane round to the left or to the right. This final section is about becoming a long-haul leader; i.e. **leading for longevity** and leaving a lasting legacy.

You'll find you are naturally better suited to one "way of moving." Some people are good at leading themselves, but they find leading others more challenging, for example. The more you "move" in the three different dimensions, the easier each will become for you.

For each theme – **leading yourself, leading others** and **leading for longevity** – there are three words that begin with the letter "H." These are the nine needs to lift-off, lead and secede in your dream. They are arranged in the shape of a plane and you'll find this diagram at the front of the book.

Finally, every chapter ends with a *Frequent Flyer* checklist, so you can return to the book at any time and quickly refresh your memory.

Okay, I'm in.

If you're still reading, then you're more determined than most dreamers. And you've chosen the right book. The chapters that follow will show you how to turn your dream into a reality and help you become someone whose life others will draw inspiration from. It will teach you to tackle the distractions, disappointments and dangers that come your way and show you how to overcome obstacles, both internal and external, until you arrive safely at your "Someday" destination. And if you have the courage and character to finish this book, then you'll uncover the lost leadership secret that's hidden in the sub-title; a profound mystery that very few people are able to comprehend and wield to their advantage: the meaning of the word "*secede*".

This isn't a book for people seeking to "get rich quick" or to exploit others for personal gain. It's about bringing others with you, and overcoming the challenges you will undoubtedly face, to make a lasting difference.

The world needs dreamers right now. Isn't it time you made "someday" today?

*Hope knocked at the door
and Faith sat down,
by Major Trust.*

Chapter 2
THE PLANE PARABLE

One question consumed the little plane:

"Where am I going?"

In the early years, the plane was content just flying with friends. They all dreamed of soaring off into the clouds. Then, one by one they did just that, until the little plane was left alone.

"You can't learn to fly on the ground," said a friendly voice.

The plane turned around to see a pilot in the hangar.

"I'm Major Trust. Permission to board?"

"I'm not ready," said the plane.

"You will be, once you start."

The pilot sat in the flight deck and they talked about a destination together. The plane wanted to go someplace warm, an island with turquoise water and white sandy beaches.

So, Major Trust set the Heading for this dream destination.

"That's a long, long way," worried the plane. "What if I don't make it?"

"You need to trust yourself and trust me. We'll get there."

As the plane taxied out, a small crowd of people were waiting by the runway.

"They heard where we're going," explained the pilot. "They want to come too."

Among the passengers was a little girl called Hope and her mother, Faith.

With so many passengers in the cabin, it took a huge effort to get the wheels moving. Finally, the plane picked up speed and gathered momentum.

The runway felt fast and unfamiliar.

"Pitch up," said the pilot. "Raise your nose!"

To the plane's astonishment and relief, it lifted off the tarmac and soared into the clouds.

"Just focus on that first landmark. We'll do one leg at a time," said the pilot, reassuringly.

After a while, the plane felt tired.

"This is hard, and it's boring!"

"Yes, it is. But it's also worth it," said the pilot. "You have to keep doing the same things, hour after hour. Keep flying straight, stay on course, stop and rest after every leg. Very slowly, you will get closer to the destination."

As the plane looked down at shiny things on the ground, it began to veer off course and lose altitude. All of a sudden, a jagged mountain range seemed to appear out of nowhere.

"Help me!"

"Calm down now. Just keep drawing air into your engines and remember those routines," said the pilot. "Fly straight, stay on course, and rest when you can. These habits will get you clear."

"I'm scared."

"Look away from the ground; keep your nose up."

As the plane approached the mountain, the pilot leaned in, "What you need now is mettle. You can do this!"

"I'm made of metal!"

"I mean, you need courage – heart."

The plane strained every rivet and pushed its engines up to full throttle, until they shook. Slowly, the plane began to climb higher, clearing the mountain tops – just in time.

"I messed up. It's too hard. I'm failing at this!" sobbed the plane.

"That just means you're learning," replied the pilot. "It's not supposed to be easy."

After a little while, the flight began to get bumpy.

Sidewinds buffeted the plane and dark clouds enveloped its fuselage.

The plane struggled to keep level, rolling left and right.

"We're flying through a storm!" one of the passengers cried out.

Soon most of the passengers were panicking. They felt angry with the plane.

"Just land. I've changed my mind."

"I want to get off. This must be the wrong way."

"This destination isn't worth the risk."

"We're going to crash! I want to leave."

But two of the passengers walked calmly towards the flight deck; Hope knocked at the door and Faith sat down, by Major Trust.

Faith reassured the plane, "I know you're scared, but look out the window: we're still on course. Planes are built to withstand lightning. Everything will be okay. We will make it to the destination. It'll all be worth it once we arrive."

The plane felt grateful and peaceful.

Then Faith's joyful daughter, Hope, asked if she could speak to the passengers over the tannoy. The plane agreed.

Hope told happy stories about the dream destination. She reminded the passengers why they came onboard in the first place:

"We'll be there soon. The beaches will be golden and the sun will be warm on our faces. There will be a beautiful view for everyone. It'll be wonderful."

Hope's stories encouraged the passengers and calmed them down. So, they agreed to stay onboard a little longer.

As the plane flew higher, climbing above the storm, it encountered some turbulence.

The passengers began to complain:

"The sun is too bright, I can't sleep."

"You spilled my drink!"

"I'm cold."

"I'm hungry."

At first, the plane lost its temper. It had worked hard to get above the storm, yet the passengers were still unhappy. Why weren't they more grateful?

"Maybe you shouldn't have come! We've been flying for a long time and my engines are tired. I have enough to do without this extra pressure. Please be quiet!"

Sadly, the plane's harsh reply only made things worse. More passengers began to grumble.

The plane felt a little lost.

"Well, what do you want me to do? I'm trying my best. How can I make you happy?"

Every passenger seemed to have a different suggestion:

"Slow right down."

"Change direction."

"Try flying really close to the ground."

"Just land. Then, we'll make a new plan."

The plane was left feeling sad and even more confused.

Then came one final suggestion, from the pilot this time.

"Try moving the flaps by your wing tips."

"I've not used them before," the plane pondered.

"They'll help you stabilise things," Major Trust explained.

Wiggling the flaps on each wing, with a little practice and patience, the plane found it could keep level and smooth things out.

"That's better!" the plane sighed, feeling relieved.

"I know it's been a bumpy ride recently. How's everyone feeling?" asked the plane.

It took time to listen to the passengers and seek to understand what was upsetting them.

"I hear that some of you are cold, some are hungry and you're all tired because it's too bright to sleep up here. Is that right?"

The passengers nodded. They felt heard.

"I understand why you're cross. But if I'd slowed down too much and flown closer to the mountains, what do you think would have happened?"

"We could have crashed," one passenger admitted. The others seemed shocked.

"We'd be flying through thick fog," the plane explained. "And we're not clear of the mountains yet. So, yes, that would be too dangerous. I want to keep you all safe."

"Is there anything else we could try? I'm sure we can solve these problems together."

The passengers had some good ideas which they were more than willing to share now that the plane was showing kindness and understanding.

"We could swap seats, it's warmer back here," one passenger proposed.

"I could share my meal," said another.

"And I've found some eye masks. I'll start handing those out."

"Could you give us a little warning the next time there's turbulence, and we'll stay belted in our seats? That's all we ask. Just keep talking to us," another person added.

The plane thanked the passengers for their suggestions and agreed.

"Well done," said the pilot. "Now your passengers are playing their part and helping us to get to the destination. It's not all up to you."

The plane felt pleased that it didn't have to change direction, fly too low, or slow down now.

Just then, it noticed one passenger was still looking cross and even discouraging the others. It could hear them saying, "This is still the wrong destination. We should turn back while we can."

That's when the pilot gave one final piece of advice, "I think you should ask this passenger to leave when we stop for fuel. If they can't agree with your destination, it's better for everyone if they find a new plane with a different heading."

At the next stopover, the problem passenger disembarked and went their own way.

After that, things went well for many miles. The plane would fly day and night, resting regularly and refuelling during planned stops.

Sunset was always the plane's favourite time as the whole sky filled with colour.

The plane would chase the sun across the horizon then gaze up at the stars at nightfall.

Flying at night was peaceful and quiet. The plane loved the way the moonlight shimmered on lakes and the starlight danced on the seas below.

One night, the plane spotted a glinting object darting across the sky.

"What was that?"

"It's the space station," the pilot answered.

"Why can't I fly up there? I should be up there! I've got the hang of this now. After all, the higher I climb, the faster I can fly!"

The pilot tried to warn the plane, explaining the air would be too thin. But it wouldn't listen.

The plane began to climb steeply, pushing both engines to full power.

Passengers came bursting into the flight deck, "What are you doing? You're going too high. You have to stop this!"

"No! I can do this! In fact, I've done it before. I do it all the time!"

The pilot sat quietly, with a sad and knowing expression.

Suddenly, the engines cut out.

The plane lost control and started to spiral down.

"I'm sorry, I do need your help!"

So, Major Trust leant forward and took hold of the controls.

Gently but firmly, the pilot lowered the nose and used the tail flaps to level the plane out. The engines roared back into life and, gradually, the plane saw the horizon come back into view; even catching a glimpse of the dream destination far off in the distance.

"Now – slowly – increase your altitude," advised the pilot.

The plane felt ashamed; both for lying and for putting everyone in danger.

It resolved to do better. From now on honesty and humility would be its guiding lights.

The plane became even more determined to fly everyone safely to the dream destination.

It fixed its heading and practised all the habits the pilot had taught: flying straight, staying on course and stopping for rests. Even when it got tired or bored, the plane showed grit and heart, refusing to give up.

Hope and Faith would visit often, to talk and have fun. And what began as hard work soon became second nature. The plane was enjoying the journey so much, it even began to wish it could last forever.

Then one day, quite unexpectedly, the journey came to an end.

"Time to lower the landing gear my friend. We've arrived," said the pilot softly.

Rather than feeling happy, the plane felt low. As it descended, it switched on three bright landing lights, signalling it was coming in to land.

It took all the plane's strength to slow down before it touched down on the concrete with a jarring bump.

As the passengers walked away from the plane they smiled and thanked it for bringing them to such a beautiful destination. Hope and Faith waved as they left, hand in hand.

"But what will I do now?"

Major Trust paused, took a long deep breath and then smiled.

"You move on. We've arrived. You're not a destination — you're a plane. It's time for you to rest, refuel and set a new heading."

The plane watched the passengers disappear into the terminal. Then glanced up at the sky, giving out a sigh.

"Okay. But let's leave tomorrow."

As the plane crawled into the hangar, it was surprised to see three other planes there waiting.

"We heard you were moving on. So, we were wondering..." the first said.

"...could you show us where you came from and how you got here?" another added.

"We'd be honoured to fly your passengers home. If you'll show us how," said the third.

PART 1

"PITCH"

LEADING YOURSELF

You see, the real problem with dreams is, we think they're too good to be true.

Chapter 3
FLIGHT DECK: HEADING
Discover your Dream Destination

*"You can have the best plane in the world,
but without a destination, it's as good as useless."*
Arnold Schwarzenegger

Hollywood actor, world champion bodybuilder
and former Governor of California

It's all about belief.

Jim Carey wrote a cheque for $10,000,000. He actually made it out to himself, as payment for "acting services." Then he folded the cheque up and kept it in his wallet for many years.

This was Jim Carey's way of saying, "I believe, one day I'll earn millions of dollars for a film." When he wrote the cheque, he was just starting out as an actor. But he had this dream destination in his sights. The cheque was a daily reminder of his lofty goal and a tangible way to visualise his dream to become a Hollywood movie star, able to command eye-watering fees. Every time he opened his wallet, that folded piece of paper kept him accountable to the "heading" he had set – like a pilot checking the instruments to ensure they're still flying in the right direction for their desired destination.

It's interesting how often you hear successful people, like Arnold Schwarzenegger, imploring dreamers to put up posters of their heroes; anything that will act as a daily reminder of your hopes and goals. Schwarzenegger says, *"Every day when you wake up, you look at those pictures and they motivate you. Every day as you work hard you can smile, as you get one step closer to turning that vision into reality."*

The comedian Michael McIntyre shares that he would drive past vast theatres and huge auditoriums and visualise his name up in lights above the doors. Some years later, he performed to thousands inside those same venues.

This isn't magic or some cosmic formula for "manifesting" thoughts into reality. The truth is far more ordinary and practical: By having something visual and tangible to serve as a daily reminder of your goal, it'll help you stay focussed on achieving your dream and, more importantly, it will begin to grow your *own* belief that it will really happen one day.

You see, the real problem with dreams is, we think they're too good to be true. We don't dare to believe they could actually happen. Instead, we're content to consign our longings, and perhaps even our calling, to a far off non-specific timeframe called "Someday."

But, since you're reading this book, you've already taken the decision to make "Someday" today. You're taxiing down the runway, ready to lift off. You're ready to go somewhere new, exciting and rewarding.

Now, to discover your dream destination and build the belief to arrive, there are three parts to setting your "Heading":

1. Let Major Trust be Your Pilot

2. Destination and Navigation

3. Pitch Your Dream

1. Let Major Trust be your Pilot

Sadly, it's not enough to have a vague dream that you'll probably pursue "Someday."

There's no shortage of people with big dreams in our world.

What's rare is individuals with enough belief and confidence to turn their dream into a reality. Even fewer display the discipline and sheer determination it takes to pursue a dream, and we'll explore this in the next chapter.

To begin with, let's look at "leading yourself." Having the right mindset, of *trust-based-on-faith,* is what it really takes to lift off before you can think about leading anyone else.

This is more than a positive mental attitude.

The first of the nine needs is the word "Heading," because getting to a dream destination means getting your *head* right first.

Henry Ford, founder of the Ford Motor Company, famously said: "Whether you think you can or whether you think you can't – you're right."

To lift off the ground, first you have to *believe* you can fly.

To put it another way, you have to have faith.

We get the word "faith" from the Latin word "*fid,*" meaning "*trust.*" It can still be found in words like "con**fid**ence," "con**fid**ential" and "con**fid**e." C*onfiding* in someone to keep something *confidential,* requires you to have *faith* in them: that you can *trust* them to keep your *confidence.*

"Fid" is also found in "**fid**elity."

When couples get married, they make trust-based promises to one another. These vows commit newlyweds to lifelong and reciprocal responsibilities: both to be faithful themselves but also to *trust, based-on-faith,* that their partner will be faithful in return. In short, *trust* is a two-way street.

"Trust" always requires a degree of faith and reciprocity; faith in our own ability to do something as well as faith in someone else that they'll do their part.

To achieve any dream you have to be piloted by *faith-based trust* – in God, in yourself and in other people. Without trust as your pilot you can't go anywhere that matters, change anything that matters or achieve anything that matters.

"Major Trust" is the pilot that will ultimately get you airborne. Trust will also keep you on course.

When trust becomes a bigger force in your life than the drag of doubt against you and downward force of reasonable fears and busyness, that's when you'll finally pull up and take off. When "I want to" becomes "I will," "I should" becomes "I shall" and "I believe in this" becomes "I believe in this enough to start" – that's when you lift off and start flying.

When it comes to achieving your dream, you have to have faith that it can happen.

Enough doubting! No more excuses. Banish fear with your faith. Believe it can be done.

You have to have confidence, and that comes from trusting yourself and others.

"Major Trust" runs like a thread through this book: trust in the dream destination and why it matters, trust in yourself to grow and take others there, trust in a Higher Power to help you, trust in the team around you and trust that you'll actually make it. Trust is how you get started, how you keep going and how you reach your destination.

So, let Major Trust be your pilot.

2. Destination and Navigation

Imagine you're setting off on a long journey to go somewhere you'll love.

What would you need to do?

- Choose your destination and the *purpose* of your trip.

- Plan your route, with stops along the way.

- Work out the cost and how long it will take.

When setting a dream "Heading," the process is much the same:

- You need to decide on your destination and *why* you want to get there. Set a clear purpose.

- You need a plan to get you there, including stops to check you're on course and to celebrate your progress.

- You need to weigh up what it will cost you (and those close to you) in time, money, sleep and other sacrifices.

A lot has been written on how to find purpose, and how to make your dreams come true.

But the truth is, this is often a lifelong pursuit. Life is made up of many journeys and happiness is never found in one destination. So, don't feel too much pressure to find the "one destination" in life that will make all your dreams come true.

Instead, aim to add value to other people's lives, to make a difference doing something you love to do, that's a pretty good place to start. There are a growing number of research studies that show living with a sense of purpose will even help you live longer.

As human beings, we're hardwired for meaning. We long for purpose. We want to belong to a community that's making a difference; to find a tribe to call home, with kindred spirits who share our hopes, dreams and values; and to spend our lives on something that matters.

Dr Martin Luther King Jr. said, "If a man or woman doesn't discover something they would be willing to die for, they are not fit to live."

The tricky part is figuring out where to start.

Many people have a dream, like Dr Martin Luther King Jr., but few figure out why this destination matters (their purpose) or make a plan to get there. Even fewer count the cost and consider the sacrifices this journey will require of them.

Some say you should look at what you're good at doing, what you love to do and what you can get paid to do, then combine those three to create your purpose. There are two issues with this rationale. Firstly, what if you don't want to do that? For example, you might want to keep what you enjoy doing as your hobby, so that it brings you life and refreshment. As soon as it becomes your job, the fun and joy drains from it. Secondly, most dreams that matter don't start with a person's personal mix of skills and pastimes.

I can't imagine the suffragettes starting their movement to win the vote with a thought shower session, "Okay, I'm good at being ridiculed and disenfranchised, and I really like prison food, I just need to get some crowd-funding now." Or could you conceive Martin Luther King Jr. workshopping some "dreams" to find out which would resonate well with crowds in Washington DC?

In today's world of data analytics and glossy social media, being led by your heart into uncharted, dangerous, unpopular or difficult territory goes against the flow of the cultural current.

How to Find Purpose:

A dream alone won't suffice. Most people have dreams that never come to anything. What you actually need is a "purpose" to drive you.

Finding purpose starts with diagnosing a genuine problem. It begins with a deep conviction inside of you that there's somewhere better out there: a better way, a different landscape, a beautiful place to find, and a worthy and challenging road to get there.

Rather than asking: What am I good at? What's fun? What's lucrative? And how can I combine them?

Instead, ask yourself these three questions:

- **What am I *Passionate* about?**

- **What *Problem* or *Pain* do I long to see solved?**

- **Who could I *Partner* with to solve it?**

These are the kinds of questions that world-changers and justice-seekers have asked themselves for centuries.

Let's take them one by one...

What am I *Passionate* about?

Your driving PASSION might simply be your idea for a better world, town, school or company. Or your PASSION could be an activity, sport or hobby; something you love to spend your time doing. You don't have to be the "best" at it. Perhaps you're still learning. That's okay.

What passions or talents would you like to invest in developing further?

Don't be too modest. What do other people say they are grateful for, when you use your knowledge or gifts to help them? What has someone asked you to help them with in the past?

In other words, what hobbies or skills are you working on, which could be useful to others?

Almost any passion can be used to help other people: music, sports, writing, prompt engineering, coding, design, public speaking, research, science, etc. The list is endless.

What *Problem* or *Pain* do I long to see solved?

With conglomerates sprawling across the globe, you'd be forgiven for thinking you are too small and insignificant to make a dent in the big problems facing our world. This is simply not true. Often big, well-funded organisations are slow to act and accountable to the wrong people. If one little girl skipping school with a cardboard placard can spark a global movement for climate change, then you can certainly make a difference.

We have AI chatbots and smartphones when what we need is human communication and emotional intelligence.

In the 21st century, we're no closer to solving the same old causes of pain, misery and suffering:

Poverty

Hunger

Injustice

Disease

Slavery

War

And to these old foes, with all our technology and advanced knowledge, we've only added to our woes:

The Climate Crisis

Water scarcity

Displaced people

Institutional racism

Deforestation

Addiction

Debt

While millions of children are still going to bed hungry, people are trafficked across borders and life-saving drugs are out of reach for the sick, the world will need people like you to speak up, act and dream big dreams of a better future.

In recent years, crisis and turmoil have become "the new normal"; social change, political change and economic change are all accelerating. The gap – the chasm – between rich and poor is growing deeper and wider, faster than ever. As a result, we are living in the age of activists, like #JustStopOil, #metoo and #BlackLivesMatter.

In Japanese, the word for crisis has two parts, "danger" (as you'd expect), but also "opportunity." If you see a problem in your community, or pain in someone's life, whether near or far, then step up and do your part to change something. There's always an opportunity to make a difference in the face of any adversity.

Ask yourself:

- What pain or problem brings out an emotional response for me?

- What injustice really breaks my heart?

- What do I really care about?

- What causes move me the most?

- What news stories or local issues would I like to help with?

- How has my own story opened my eyes to a specific inequality or injustice?

Remember, every charity, business, book, every website, venture and community project starts as someone's "dream to solve a problem."

Elon Musk once said, "You get paid in direct proportion to the difficulty of problems you solve." The more important the need, the more valuable the dream to solve it.

Many people are searching for a meaningful dream to pursue. But it starts with the needs of others, not with your needs and desires. It starts with seeing a Painful Problem, using your Passion to do something about it, and then, lastly, identifying some Partners to help you.

Who could I *Partner* with to solve it?

Anyone can make a difference and use their Passion to help tackle a big problem; no matter how "small" you feel and whether you are young or old, black, brown or white, rich or poor.

But history's world-changers and power-shakers all have one thing in common: they never do it alone.

Greta Thunberg wouldn't have been invited to speak to world leaders if she was the only truant schoolgirl with a placard. And if Rosa Parks was the only activist refusing to give up her seat to a white person, we probably wouldn't know her as the mother of the civil rights movement.

Dreamers become leaders when they enlist the help of others. When they join a community that shares their values and together they grow in their belief that the status quo *can* change.

For your dream solution to a problem to become a reality you'll always need Partners; people whose hearts break over the same issue as yours does. Look for a like-minded community. When you do meet and dream with others – with your tribe – you'll find they have different but complementary passions, skills and resources.

Partners come in many different guises: they could be contributors, patrons, customers, audiences, supporters, investors, donors, social media followers, sports clubs, enthusiast groups, even professional unions or advocacy communities. They could bring financial resources or no money at all. Perhaps they'll bring essential knowledge or sheer hard work.

Don't only look to "take," as a Partner to others, consider what you can "give." Remember, you have experiences, interests and relationships in a unique combination, unlike anyone who has ever lived on our planet. Your story is unique and so the difference you can make in the world is unique. You have potential to help change things. And others need your help, input and contribution to change things too.

So, who could be *your* Partners?

Who shares your values? Who can you ask to help make your dream solution possible? Who believes in you or has similar hopes for the future?

And since every dream comes at a cost, and every purpose has a price-tag, who could help pay for it? Who might donate towards it? Who could invest in it?

Just watch out for motives. Some people look like good partners on the surface, but they may be driven by other ambitions and darker dreams of their own. These people make for very bad partners as they will undermine your goal in the long run. Go with a pure heart over a blank cheque every time when choosing your Partners.

If your own Passion happens to make money, who could you bless with a donation or investment? Perhaps finance or gifts-in-kind are what you can bring to the table.

Whatever Passion you bring to the Problem, however rare your skills or valuable your resources, you will need to work with Partners. It's only through partnership that a dream and solution will happen.

So, ask yourself:

- What knowledge, skills or time do I have to offer?

- What relationships or influence do I have?

- In what ways can I help the poor by partnering with others?

- What ideas do I have which could add value to a community?

- What assets do I possess that people could benefit from?

- Do I have something to offer a community project, business, charity or advocacy group to help improve people's lives?

Now, draw three circles, one for each:

PASSION?

PROBLEM?

PARTNERS?

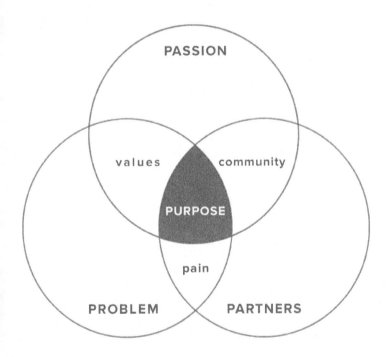

Using this template (see diagram), you can write down your thoughts inside the three circles, noting your answers to the questions we've considered for each heading.

Then, in the middle of the circles, simply write PURPOSE.

You'll see from the diagram, where *Partners* and *Passion* intersect you will find your like-minded "community."

Where the *Problem* and your *Passion* intersect, you will be motivated by guiding "values" and your belief system.

Finally, the *Problem* and your *Partners* intersect because you are united by the same "pain" and the same cause, to solve a need or injustice. You and your *Partners* may be moved by the plight of others or you may be experiencing similar challenges personally and so seek to overcome them together, combining your different strengths, gifts and passions.

By joining (or by gathering) a community that shares your values, you can Partner with others and use your Passion – something you love doing – to solve a Problem that causes pain.

Creating Your Purpose Statement:

Once you've written some answers in each of the three circles: Passion, Problem and Partners then you're ready to build these into your Purpose Statement.

Your Purpose Statement will drive you. It will get you up early and help you keep going, even when you're tired and fed up. It will fuel you with optimism, energise you and propel you forward every day.

By writing your dream down as a Purpose Statement, you'll remind yourself why it matters and who you are helping.

So, next, we'll use this simple 'I-With-So' model to build your Purpose Statement:

"I ... [PASSION: a specific activity] ..." – write this in the *present tense* drawing on one or more of your skills and talents.

"with ... [PARTNERS: people and organisations] ..." – a reminder that you need others to achieve your dream and they need you to achieve their dream.

"so ... [PROBLEM: a need or injustice you want to rectify] ..." – adding "*so*" spells out the difference you will make in other people's lives. Always phrase this as a *positive solution*.

Your Purpose Statement should never be selfish, it should be selfless.

Keep it as punchy and concise as you possibly can.

Here's what your Purpose Statement could look like:

I lead a running club *(Passion)*

with friends who live locally, *(Partners)*

so my community can stay healthy. *(Problem)*

I record a monthly podcast

with guests who share my passion for fighting climate change,

so more people understand the need to protect our planet.

I play in a band that records new songs

with support from local radio and music festivals,

so the justice issues we care about reach a national audience.

I provide hot meals and advice for homeless people

with funding and support from our community,

so, one day, nobody will sleep rough on the streets of our city.

You may find you need to re-work your phrases a few times to remove superfluous words. For example:

"I run a charity that seeks to provide one hot nutritious meal per day and pro-bono legal advice on all aspects of tenancy and local government aid."

This can be shortened to,

"I provide hot meals and advice for homeless people."

You can always add the extra details on a leaflet, poster or website. If you're writing for an organisation or on behalf of a group, just replace the word "I" with "We," e.g.

"We provide hot meals and advice for homeless people."

Be ruthless and disciplined, keeping your Purpose Statement as short, succinct and memorable as possible. A good rule of thumb is that you should be able to recite it from memory one week after you've finished writing it.

Finally, never follow "I" with the words "...am the."

For example, don't say:

"I *am* the fastest person on a running track in my country."

The reason? Your vision is not your identity.

If you're an athlete, for example, you should instead say:

I pursue personal bests as an athlete

with coaches who motivate me and teammates to train alongside,

so others are inspired to believe they can achieve great things.

In this second version, you're only competing against yourself, and you're doing it to benefit others and help them improve their own lives. The motive is selfless not purely selfish. This version isn't about beating people for the rest of your life, it's about inspiring others and leaving a legacy behind, beyond your own personal bests and boasts.

My point is, your dream can be your calling and even the focus of your life's work, but it is separate from *who* you are. *You* are not *what you do.* You are not *what you want to see happen.* You have value and intrinsic worth as a human being, before you pick up a brush to paint, send a single email, or sing a solitary note. What you create or make happen is worth celebrating and worth your effort, but don't create something hoping it will fill a hole in your soul. It won't. Ever.

If you live to be the greatest, the best, the fastest, the strongest, or the *first* anything, you'll be sorely disappointed. This is an exhausting and almost impossible feat to maintain, so you'll end up feeling a failure. Even Usain Bolt could only be the "fastest" runner on earth for a few years, until he was regularly beaten. The worth of his "soul" wasn't measured by the speed of his "soles."

Know that your Purpose Statement is not "who" you are; it's something you are working towards. Your Purpose Statement is a tool; it's not a secret route to happiness or inner fulfilment. Your dream is something you do and pursue, to add value to someone else. Don't define yourself by whether or not you achieve it.

Your Purpose Statement will, however, help you to distil your vague hopes and nebulous ideas into one meaningful sentence. Your dream destination will come into crystal clear focus as a *purpose*, and this purpose can then easily be turned into a step-by-step *plan*.

Before we move on to the plan, take a moment to imagine what it would look like, if you and your partners succeed in everything you set out to do in your Purpose Statement.

Fast forward three, five or even ten years in your mind. Think big!

If you had a time machine and could bring footage back from the future, what would we see? How will you have changed as a person? Who are the people around you? And how will life be different for the people you're trying to help when you do solve that big Problem?

Picture your Purpose Statement being fully and perfectly achieved in ten years' time – this will give you a "Vision" of the future. This, ultimately, is your "someday dream."

Your "vision" is simply a clear mental picture of your preferred future; something you could describe to an artist and they would then be able to draw for you. This vision will help you stay locked on your "Heading."

Now that you have your Purpose Statement, you know the *purpose* of your trip. Your vision will give you an inspiring and sustaining picture of where you're trying to get to and what it will be like when you finally arrive. It reminds you it'll be worth all the work.

As with any long journey, the next thing you need is to plan: a route to your dream destination with strategic stops along the way.

Plan Your Stops

"A goal without a plan is just a wish."
Antoine de Saint-Exupéry

Airlines break long-haul flights down into more manageable legs. They add practical stops along the flight-plan to refuel and change crews. In the same way, you need to plan some "stops" to *check you're still on course* and to *celebrate the progress* you're making.

Your plan will help you navigate to your end destination. All you need to do is break your big "Purpose Statement" goal down into five to ten mini-goals along the way. These are like stepping stones along your path. Each time you reach one, you can celebrate with others and you'll know you're still on track to reach the final destination.

Make sure you choose mini goals that are measurable. In other words, you should be one hundred per cent sure when a mini goal can be ticked off your list. For example, instead of "look for a good venue," choose a mini goal that can be answered with a simple "yes" or "no." Something more like this: *"The venue is chosen and paid for"* ... *tick, yes!*

Next, check your mini goals are in the right order, then you can write an "achieve by" date next to each one.

Setting dates for each leg of your plan will tell you if you're slipping behind on your plan, or if you're going to need more time and most likely more money.

Finally, write a *To Do* list under each of your mini goals. These "Tiny Tasks" are the final piece of the jigsaw puzzle. Without a detailed list of practical "actions" even your mini goals may seem daunting and unachievable. Often these Tiny Tasks will include learning a new skill or asking someone else for help, as your "WITH" Partners will often have experience and skills that you lack.

Here's a quick illustration, using one I-WITH-SO example from earlier:

Purpose Statement

I lead a running club **with** friends who live locally, **so** my community can stay healthy.

Mini Goals

- Club name and logo chosen: by 1 March

- Vision and Rules of Club written down: 15 March

- Club Facebook Page has 30 members: by 1 May

- 5+ people booked on the first run: by 10 May

- First successful run is complete: by 17 May

Tiny Tasks

Club name and logo chosen: by 1 March

- Susie and Dwaine asked for name ideas ☐ (tick box)

- Uploaded brief to the logo designer's website ☐

- Paid for final logo ☐

Vision and Rules of Club written down: by 15 March

- Vision written out ☐ (tick box)

- Rules and risks researched online ☐

- Permission checked with the land owner ☐

- Risk Assessment complete ☐

- Rules compared with established running clubs ☐

- Rules written down ☐

And so on, for each of the mini goals.

By breaking your Purpose Statement down into a timeline of Mini Goals, then breaking this down further into a "To Do" list of Tiny Tasks, your huge dream will suddenly seem possible. You have a roadmap to get you from where you are now to where you'd love to be.

When you put all this together, your action plan will be ready, plotting out the route ahead.

Every time you achieve one of your Mini Goals, be sure to "stop and celebrate," whether alone or with a team. These Mini Goals are your milestones. They are landmarks on your long journey. As you pass each Mini

Goal, be encouraged; you're getting closer to your dream destination and making progress!

Not everything will go smoothly since no plan survives impact with life's unforeseen events. But now you have your "map." When you wander off or deviate from this preferred path, you can always get back on track eventually, by looking out for your next landmark.

If you find yourself getting demoralised and stuck on "Tiny Tasks," lift your eyes back up to the horizon: your Purpose Statement. And do something to bring your "longer view" vision back into crystal clear focus. Recall afresh how amazing it'll feel to achieve your dream.

3. Pitch your Dream to others

So, how do you get others onboard with your vision?

Saying your dream out loud, to actual human beings, always feels scary and vulnerable. But there is a proven way to find people who share your heart for a problem, enlisting partners to journey towards a solution with you.

Successful leaders pitch vision by painting a vivid picture of their dream destination in the imagination of their hearers: You have to describe what your vision will *look like* one day, both the big, long-view (time machine) vision and the small "SO" from your Purpose Statement. Then you invite people to partner with you on this adventure. You can write it down, record it as a video or put on an event. But you'll need to "pitch" your dream to others eventually.

Arguably the most famous "dream" in history was "pitched" by Rev. Dr Martin Luther King Jr. on 28 August 1963 when Dr King stood on the steps of the Lincoln Memorial and painted his powerful and vivid picture of the future.

"I have a dream that one day this nation... will live out the true meaning of its creed: all men are created equal.. I have a dream that one day even the state of Mississippi will be transformed into an oasis of freedom and justice."

This is the "so" part of Dr King's Purpose Statement. The difference he wants to see made in other people's lives, phrased as a positive solution.

He goes on to describe the vision, depicting what it will look like on a *small* day to day scale: "...little black boys and black girls will be able to join hands with little white boys and white girls as sisters and brothers. I have a dream today." This is a scene you can visualise in your mind. You could even draw it. And here's another: "...one day the sons of former slaves and the sons of former slave owners will be able to sit down together at the table of brotherhood." You could draw the table and the chairs and you can picture this scene, like a painting.

Dr King also spells out his inspiring and moving dream on a *big* scale, his long-view vision: "I have a dream that my four little children will one day live in a nation where they will not be judged by the colour of their skin but by the content of their character."

This is also how he concludes his pitch, with the larger "time machine" vision: "... Black men and white men, Jews and Gentiles, Protestants and Catholics, will be able to join hands and sing: 'Free at last. Free at last. Thank God Almighty, we are free at last.'"

Martin Luther King Jr. weaves micro scenes and macro pictures together, to paint a vivid picture of his dream – to end the pain and problem of racial injustice. His visual pictures helped this speech resonate down the decades and made it memorable.

Finally, even in a speech to over 250,000 people, you hear Dr King invite others along for the journey. He asks them to trust and partner with him: "With this faith we'll be able to work together, to pray together, to struggle together, to go to jail together, to stand up for freedom together, knowing that we'll be free one day."

Dr King is not promising the road will be easy, but he's saying the destination will be worth it.

So, to win partners and get people on board with your dream to solve a painful problem, paint a vivid picture of a hopeful future with your words. Describe what your "so" will *look like*, by picking some "small" examples. Also, help people imagine what it'll look like in a few years' time, depicting the long-view vision on a big scale. Then, invite them to join you on the journey to get there, being honest about the "cost."

It'll be scary to share your vision, and to ask for help. It takes courage to entrust your dream to others, to con*fide* in them and ask them to trust you. In the next section we'll look at how we muster that courage.

Frequent Flyer

- To lift off the ground, first you just have to believe you can fly.

- Be piloted by Major **Trust** – in God, in yourself and in other people.

- Without Trust as your pilot, you can't go anywhere that matters, change anything that matters or achieve anything that matters.

- Finding purpose starts with diagnosing a genuine problem. Start with your Passion and a Painful Problem, then identify some Partners to help.

- Write your "I-WITH-SO" **Purpose** Statement. Keep it short and memorable. Avoid the "I am..." trap.

- Do the time machine exercise: picture yourself in five or ten years' time: that's your dream destination and your **vision** of the preferred future.

- Make an action **plan** for how to get to that future; breaking it down into smaller Mini Goal stepping stones, each with Tiny Tasks.

- **Pitch** the vision by painting big and small pictures of the dream destination you imagine in future, then invite people to partner with you despite the cost.

"The soul never thinks without a picture." – Aristotle

THE PLANE PARABLE

Failure is how you grow and mistakes are how you learn.

Chapter 4
ENGINES: HABITS & HEART

Do what most people won't
to get what most people don't

"People do not decide their future,
they decide their habits and their habits
decide their future."
Matthias Alexander

In most Hollywood movies, when history is made or justice dispensed, an inspirational hero gives a stirring speech set to an orchestral score that swells to a triumphant crescendo. Viewers fist-pump the air and the credits roll. Everyone lives happily ever after.

If only life were that neat, tidy and fair.

When Wilberforce finally passed the legislation to end transatlantic slavery, for instance, it wasn't a big speech that changed history. Rather, it was a little loophole hidden in some small print. And it took him over thirty years – a mite more than the usual 120 minutes we see on screen.

Every single year, from 1789 to 1806, Wilberforce put forward a bill to abolish the cruel but lucrative business of buying, selling and owning human beings: men, women and their children. And every year, he was defeated. Wilberforce failed over, and over and over again. There was even an excruciating glimmer of hope, in 1804, when the House of Commons did vote in favour of abolition, only for this landmark ruling to be overturned by the House of Lords. Can you even begin to imagine how Wilberforce must have felt in that moment? After fifteen years of futility, failure and rejection, that took a heavy toll on his health, how did he find the strength and resolve to keep going?

Two years later, a lawyer friend of Wilberforce, James Stephen, came up with a brilliant idea. He proposed that any ship that was "neutral" in the war against Napoleon, should be banned from carrying "cargo" to any part of his French empire.

What seemed like a patriotic and straight-forward law to help the war effort, served to cut down the ships carrying "human cargo," reducing the slave trade by two-thirds. A decisive blow that marked the beginning of the end.

In 1807, after more relentless campaigning, Parliament finally bowed to public pressure and passed a bill explicitly outlawing the transatlantic slave trade. Yet, it would take William Wilberforce and his friends a further twenty-six years of gruelling struggle and tireless work to free every person owned as property. Finally, on Friday 26 July 1833 the Emancipation Bill passed its second reading – as Wilberforce lay on his deathbed.

William Wilberforce had no way of knowing he would be successful. He didn't know how his "movie" would end. And his fight to end the trade in slaves, took a huge toll on his mental and physical health, as well as destroying his reputation.

In fact, when Wilberforce introduced his first Abolition Bill, in May 1789, he suffered slander, abuse and threats. He was even challenged to a duel to the death.

Wilberforce would not have prevailed against such fierce and formidable opposition, without being driven by his internal convictions and Christian faith. This gave him courage, an inner strength and steel; often called *Heart*. And he knew what it meant to wait. In the end, his stubborn refusal to give up was like the drip, drip, drip of water wearing away the hardest rock. What Wilberforce and his contemporaries achieved was nothing short of miraculous. His self-discipline and determination, spanning half his life, is ultimately more impressive than any of his famed three-hour speeches to Parliament. It wasn't quick-witted words that won the day, it was slow and painstaking work over three decades. This takes the kind of stamina and consistency that can only be achieved through disciplined *Habits*.

There are no shortage of people with a Someday Dream, but how many people are living like they'll achieve it?

Discipline is what's needed to "show up" and keep moving towards your dream. To consistently make progress, day after day, despite demoralising disappointments, sheer tiredness and the temptation to take an easier path or a short cut.

How do you maintain discipline? The answer is "Habits."

Progress requires disciplined Habits. You have to keep doing the basics, over and over. The way you move a mountain is one shovel at a time. Every day, you work hard and move all the earth you can, and every day you move just a little closer to your goal. Every day, you make some progress. To achieve any goal that matters, you've got to have self-discipline. Success takes time and rugged determination. It takes continuous, often monotonous, effort. This is why many successful leaders have similar habits and daily routines; they get up early, make time to exercise and read books to learn and grow.

It's not enough to have talent. It's what you do with the talent that counts. A great idea that stays on paper can be outdone by a mediocre idea that's put into action. Even the most gifted people, born innovators and natural leaders, can squander their potential and limit their impact through lack of discipline and application.

The book won't write itself – you have to set aside the hours to write. The sports club won't happen unless you get the equipment out each week and send reminders. That new community project won't magically spring into being unless you share your vision with others.

"Our lives are fashioned by our choices.
First we make our choices.
Then our choices make us."
Anne Frank

Imagine rolling a boulder: just getting the rock moving from a stationary position, even a fraction, takes a herculean effort, until momentum is built up. And if you stop pushing, all the effort is wasted and you have to start all over again.

H is for...

The "H" word for this section is "Habits," but it could just as easily have stood for "Hard work." We've got so used to world changers getting the job done in just over two hours on screen. In truth, it can take a lifetime to affect meaningful change. The bigger the problem that must be solved, the greater the effort and commitment required to do it.

Take Martin Luther King Junior as an example. We all know the spine-tingling "I have a dream" speech. But did you know it was one of Dr King's "greatest hits?" He hadn't planned to say that part, until someone shouted, "tell them about your dream!" You see Dr King had shared his dream many times, across America. On this occasion, a good speech became an iconic address when he moved into well-worn material he could recite word for word.

The truth is, getting something important done is often repetitive and unexciting, even tedious at times. You have to have the same conversation with different people, write similar letters, articles, blogs or emails, record podcasts or videos with similar themes and even turn down friends who invite you to socialise because you're too busy on your project. You may give the same talk over and over again.

People don't see the ninety per cent of the iceberg that's under the waterline; the choice to do hours of work unpaid or to read every day for at least twenty minutes; to pray each morning, to commit to learning. They just see the moments of success poking out above the water.

Deferred gratification is key to success in many aspects of life, including achieving your dream. Ever been on a diet? It's the same principle: you have to deny yourself and what you want now, to get what you want most, later.

To put it another way: you have to do what most people won't if you want to get what most people don't!

Often this means choosing your pain – the pain of regret or the pain of progress. As Jim Rohn explains, "We must all suffer one of two pains: the pain of discipline or the pain of regret. The difference is discipline weighs ounces, while regret weighs tons."

"First we make our habits, then our habits make us."
John Dryden

Human beings are creatures of habit. So, form helpful habits and repeat routines that will move you in the direction of your dreams. And work to break the less productive or unhealthy habits that are moving you further away from your dream destination.

Our lives are the sum total of how we decide to spend our time. Or, to put it another way, "we are what we repeatedly do."

Discipline is not simply having the willpower to get out of bed and go for that run – it's about consistency. Rise at 6am and write 200 words once and you've nothing much to show for it. Do that every day, for a year, and you can write a book.

This will, of course, take time. Like a plane taxiing on a runway, you'll start slowly at first, building the habit and then gradually you gather momentum and accelerate, seeing some progress. Nothing happens, until suddenly everything happens, you lift off and begin to fly.

Distraction is not your friend

One big threat to what you want to get done today, I guarantee, will be distraction. I remember watching an interview where Roald Dahl, the famous children's author, explained how he overcame distractions. He would walk to the end of his garden, where he had a little room built. He'd sit in an old comfy worn-out chair, set out some sharpened pencils, pull a tray across his lap, and settle into what he called a "nest." There, he could write for hours. Dahl found a state of being where he could create whole worlds of imagination and conjure up characters like Willy Wonka to delight millions of children.

Our world is increasingly designed to distract and even addict us. Every device "pings" and notifications demand our attention every few seconds.

But when did you last allow yourself to feel bored?

Do you ever just sit in silence, without a screen or music or a podcast blaring? When you make space, stop and shut off distractions, your brain gets to work processing problems and working on ideas in the background. Your brain's "default network" activates when you let your mind wander, during activities that don't require focussed concentration and attention. In other words, you do your best creative thinking when you rest or you're preoccupied by a mundane task that doesn't need much brain power.

So, burst through the boredom barrier. Don't take your phone out when you're waiting in a queue or sitting on a train. Go for walks and be alone with your thoughts. Have a bath without a book. Or go for a jog or swim, without wearable tech pinging you. Even the great thinker, physicist Albert Einstein, extolled the benefits of boredom, *"I think 99 times and find nothing. I stop thinking, swim in silence, and the truth comes to me."*

Out of nowhere, a little lightbulb moment will take you by surprise. Scribble it down, while it's fresh and clear in your mind. Clarity comes when you "stop thinking" and do something repetitive, without rushing to fill the silence with an entertaining distraction, like a video or voices on the radio. Allowing yourself enough uninterrupted silence to actually "feel bored" is so rare and valuable, most people don't do it, and it doesn't cost you a penny. Just be bored for a change; a change in your perspective.

> *"I count him braver, who overcomes their desires*
> *than they who conquer their enemies,*
> *for the hardest victory is over self."*
> **Aristotle**

One thing you need to know

The biggest obstacle, standing between you and your dream, is fear.

Fear will make you want to give up. Plain and simple. Habits will move you closer to success, but fear is waiting to trip you up and take you out.

It amazes me that children aren't taught how their brains and bodies react to fear while they're in school. You can fill a child's head with knowledge, hone their gifts and offer endless opportunities for the future, but if you fail to teach them what fear does to them and how to conquer it, you've wasted your time.

In fact, if learning how to be bored is a valuable quality, then learning how to calm yourself is utterly priceless!

The truth is that all your strengths and skills are irrelevant without emotional intelligence, especially the ability to reflect and then respond calmly to a threat or conflict.

We've known the power of fear for centuries. And we also know how to tame it. So, if you've not heard how to conquer your fear and feelings of panic, then these next few paragraphs may change your life:

Most of the time we're using our Prefrontal Cortex (let's call that the PFC) when we're thinking conscious thoughts, making decisions, planning ahead or problem solving. This is the front part of our brain; the region behind your forehead. Your PFC also helps you moderate your social behaviour, weigh up judgements, and predict the consequences of different responses. If someone annoys you, your PFC will help you not to punch them in the face, as this would have negative ramifications for you. In basic terms, the PFC is the "thinking" part of the brain, which gives us control over our more primitive impulses.

The problem is that there's an "override button" that puts your PFC into "Flight Mode."

You don't have a choice about this. Your brain doesn't ask your permission first.

If you're in danger, a "switch" gets tripped in our brains. When your body perceives a threat, it responds automatically. This switch can also get flipped if we feel unsafe or really worried about something. It's as if our brain says, "Look, I don't know what you're up to, but this isn't safe. I'm taking over so you survive this."

Imagine a tiger walked into the room right now. Before you can even process this threat, a tiny gland at the base of your brain, the Amygdala, fires off a chemical that makes you "JUMP" or "FREEZE." This is why you "jump," when you're surprised by someone or you watch a scary movie. This initial reaction helps you literally jump out of the way of a predator. It's also why people freeze when they try to abseil from a high building. It's hard wired, to buy us time.

Think of the Amygdala as your body's twitchy security guard. "That's fair enough," you might say. This seems like a handy feature to have pre-installed in your body's operating system.

But the next thing the Amygdala does, without consulting you, is to send a "distress signal" into a part of your brain called the "hypothalamus." This is the really annoying part. The Amygdala basically says, "You're in trouble! I'm sounding the alarm. All systems GO!"

This puts your whole body into "Boost Mode"; by activating your Sympathetic Nervous System response.

Do you remember the PFC, which helps you act rationally and make careful considered choices? This Boost Mode briefly overpowers the PFC, the thinking part of your brain. And when your PFC is in "Flight Mode," you can't think straight. Your mind feels foggy and your thoughts can race. This occurs when you're feeling scared or extremely anxious. Have you ever got up to do some public speaking, and despite rehearsing for hours, your mind goes blank? Blame your Amygdala!

So what happens to your body in Boost Mode?

The brain just wants to feel safe again and so it gets your body primed to tackle a threat.

This is better known as the "Fight or Flight" response – because that's what it's getting you ready for; to fight the tiger or literally run for your life. It sharpens your senses and prepares you for a physical confrontation.

The Amygdala floors the accelerator pedal, and you have absolutely no say in it. This pushes everything in your body up to full power, like an aeroplane throttling up for take-off from a runway.

Eyes – They widen as pupils dilate to improve your vision. Your senses are heightened.

Heart – It beats faster and so you experience palpitations, as your body primes for a fight.

Throat – It can feel constricted, as your breathing becomes more rapid, boosting blood flow.

Mouth – It goes dry as blood vessels narrow, to provide max power to your major muscles, like legs and arms.

Skin – It feels hot and cold, as your body's systems speed up and then a cold sweat cools you down for a confrontation or pursuit.

Bladder – It *relaxes*, to make you quick on your feet.

Lungs – They breath faster and your airways open up, which can make you feel light-headed.

Stomach – The blood supply diverts away from the digestive system, which feels like "butterflies" or nausea.

Do any of these sensations sound familiar?

All of these automatic "Boost Mode" systems happen very fast, which can make us feel a sense of panic. But they're actually intended to save your life.

When we are in this "fearful" state for too long because our brain perceives a threat or danger is persisting, then our body releases cortisol, which helps keep "Boost Mode" jammed on for as long as possible. This isn't good for us over a long period – staying in top gear, at full throttle, with a prolonged state of "stress" placed on our system. It can have negative effects on your health over time.

The problem is no one has upgraded the human operating system for thousands of years.

Your body only has "one card to play" and one unconscious response to danger and threats: the tried and tested boost button override, that shuts down your PFC. This automatic response to a threat is ideal for dealing with a tiger, but not so great if the thing that's causing you "stress" is a traffic jam or an email.

In truth, there's no such thing as a "stressful email" or a "stressful conversation." Stress is simply our body's response to a piece of information about "danger." By changing our thoughts about this input, we can change how our bodies respond to it.

Modern life presents so many scary challenges that cannot be solved by fighting or running away, such as alarming news headlines, public speaking, moving house, pandemics, deadlines, family tragedies, friends suffering with health issues, household bills (the list is endless).

These stressors can feel like threats, which then trigger our Boost Mode and keep it switched on for long periods. This is especially unhelpful in moments when we feel afraid. Usually, the very same moments when we'd benefit from a calm head, good judgement and careful planning. Not to mention a good night's sleep.

So, in the heat of the moment, is there a way to tell your Amygdala to chill out, because you don't need to fight or run away?

Although you cannot stop "Boost Mode" from activating, you can learn to recognise the tell-tale signs of your body's automatic response, and you can even learn to calm down.

Thankfully, our body has another "automatic system": The Parasympathetic Nervous System (also known as "Rest and Digest"). It's a bit like a brake pedal, that helps us calm down and relax, so we can think clearly again. It can actually take around one hour for adrenaline to dissipate after it's spiked, which is why it can take an hour to calm down properly and think straight if you get really angry with someone. You're not going to make good decisions when you're angry, stressed out or scared. Your brain is literally not working as it normally does. When "Rest and Digest" activates, your Amygdala relents and you regain control over your brain and body; your pupils, airways, heart, stomach and digestion all return to normal and your body releases melatonin to help you sleep and recover from the Boost Mode and recharge.

How to calm down and be B.L.E.S.T

Fear doesn't just steal your focus and inhibit your problem solving, it also saps your creativity and energy. It is physically, mentally and emotionally exhausting to remain in Boost Mode for too long. And prolonged fear can even make you unwell.

So, how can you flip the switch back to "Rest Mode" more quickly?

There are some very well documented and proven ways to turn your frontal lobe back on, so you can think clearly and feel calm again. These techniques can be grouped under the acronym B.L.E.S.T:

Breathing

Breathing – slowly in and slower out – is the primary way to tell your body that "all is well." Breathing slowly and evenly, calmly drawing air down into the lower part of your belly, then exhaling gradually over the count of four. Imagine you are inflating a balloon behind your belly button. This is the way you tell your brain, "I've got it covered. We're safe. I want to relax." Breathing slow and deep is a relaxation technique that's found in various forms of therapy, relaxation and prayer. So, if you notice your body displaying the classic signs of "Boost Mode," pause, and use this breathing exercise first, to slow things down. Unless you're actually running from a tiger, that is!

Laugh with Friends

If you're feeling stressed or anxious, seeking out social support will help to calm and soothe you. Spend time with friends or family who make you laugh, rather than those who make you feel more tensed up and worried. Laughing with friends, and also listening to uplifting or calming music, will improve your mood and outlook.

Exercise and Eat properly

Physical activity relieves stress: It improves breathing, helps blood flow and enhances your mood. When you feel pent up and stressed, then find a way to exercise. Go out for a walk around the block, or head to the gym to lift weights. Just fifteen minutes of movement every day will change your mood, especially outdoors. Exercise is a win-win for your brain and your body. It dissipates the "Boost Mode" hormones (adrenaline and cortisol) so your body can return to its rest-and-digest state *and* exercise causes the release of feel-good neurotransmitters (endorphins), which actively make you feel better. Alongside exercise, avoiding high-sugar and high-carb junk food will also help your mood. If you're feeling worried or stressed, you're more likely to grab unhealthy food on-the-go or to comfort-eat with takeaways and sweet treats. Eating fruit and healthy protein, while cutting out sweets, crisps, fries and fizzy drinks will improve your mood. It's easy to get into the cycle of feeling bad and then eating bad, which makes you feel lethargic and gives you low energy, just when exercise and eating well are what you need to feel better.

Sleep Well

Very few of us get enough quality sleep. We put our phone down moments before we lay our head down and we pick it up again as soon as we open our eyes. The blue light from small screens disrupts our sleep by suppressing the hormone melatonin. We should all be getting seven to eight hours of high-quality sleep every night, while avoiding devices and heavy meals a couple of hours before bed. Caffeine and alcohol also play havoc with your natural sleep rhythms. You may find you need to avoid tea and coffee from the late afternoon. Develop your own regular sleep pattern – winding down with a book or bath. This way, your brain gets used to recognising the "runway to rest." It's also really important to develop rhythms of rest, more broadly: a cadence of stopping to rest and refresh yourself every day, every week, every month and every year. For instance, eat your meals away from your desk and take regular breaks, perhaps going outside for a walk. And set aside one day every week that you keep work-free; the practice of a "sabbath." Ideally, use this day to do something you enjoy. A hobby that occupies your mind that's totally separate from your paid work. And finally, book in your holidays early, so you can prioritise your windows for unwinding with loved ones, spacing out these times of fun and rest across the year. This will help you stay healthy and, conversely, make you more productive.

Turn Off Triggers

Our brains respond to triggers: the threats, stressors and dangers that keep spiking our adrenaline. By turning off the repeat reminders of reasons to feel unsafe, you'll help your body to apply the "brake" and prevent the re-activation of Boost Mode, every time you try and calm down. When you've been in fight-or-flight mode, as you try to reset, your body will be more vigilant and sensitive to re-boost at the slightest sign that a tiger has returned.

Turning off the incessant reminders that trigger feelings of stress or worry, usually means changing the settings on your phone to switch off your non-urgent notifications. This includes Breaking News banners, social media notifications, email badges and instant message alerts: if it really is urgent someone will always phone you. Removing these triggers gives your brain and body a fair chance to reset and return to rest mode.

Do all you can to reduce or eliminate the daily triggers that cause you to worry. It's been said that worrying is like praying for what you don't want to happen. Instead, free up that mental capacity and your emotional resources to focus on overcoming actual challenges that you cannot avoid, as they present themselves.

When you can, intentionally delay an important decision or a potentially difficult conversation, when you sense you are feeling low, irritable or overly sleepy. First work through the BLEST steps and then, when you've rested and are thinking clearly, revisit that big meeting or problem.

Take Heart

Disciplined Habits will take you so far, keeping you calm and so clear-headed and more productive. But, the truth is, to see any dream realised it still takes a good measure of "Heart."

Some call it mettle, some courage, others resilience. Whatever word you use, it's that five per cent extra you'll need to succeed; the sheer determination and guttural doggedness leaders find, when they push through to see a breakthrough.

Heart is the most visceral and vital element of self-leading: the fortitude to keep going when you feel like giving up.

When you're pursuing a dream, you'll always reach a point when reality lands a blow that stings! Perhaps the money runs out, your fool-proof plan fails, your idea gets rejected or your team turn their back on you. When you hit this wall, you'll know.

You'll feel drained, downtrodden, demotivated, even demoralised. Your "get up and go," will feel like it's, well, "got up and gone." That's when you really have to dig deep.

Your inner monologue will search for reasons to throw in the towel:

I'm done.

It's not worth it.

Why did I think I could do this?

No one believes in me.

The timing's not right.

I can't keep going.

I give up.

Stop that.

Don't hang around feeling sorry for yourself. Yes, it's tough. Yes, it's harder than you expected. That's life. Now get up and keep moving.

Winston Churchill said it best, "When you're going through hell, keep going." In other words, don't stop in the middle of a dark and scary storm cloud. Keep going until you reach blue sky and sunlight on the other side.

Few are born with "heart," rather it's something that grows and reveals itself in a person when they're placed under pressure, knocked back by adversity or gripped by the jaws of defeat. The rugged survival expert, Bear Grylls, has pushed his body and mind to limit many times. He believes "Heart" is "a muscle we can *all* build, by walking through the pain again and again," adding, "when everything is going wrong, *give more* rather than *give up*."

It takes grit to lead; mettle to make something happen. Once the honeymoon period ends, you have to get your head down and wade through the treacle of tedium, tiredness and temptation. As wise old heads have said, these are "character building."

"Suffering produces perseverance; perseverance, character; and character, hope."
Romans 5:3-5

Perseverance and character. Grit and courage. These are the qualities a leader needs to survive leadership. This is Heart: and it's the solid rock that dreams are built on.

It's easy to think that the opposite of fear is courage, whereas it's not. The opposite of fear is faith. If you have faith in God, yourself, your team and your dream, you can overcome fear and muster the courage you need to keep going until you finish the job. In fact, it's not really courage if you're not scared at the same time. Courage can only exist when fear is present. And as Aristotle said, "you'll never do anything in this world without courage. It is the greatest quality, next to honour."

Thankfully, Heart is something you grow in over time, as you practise tenacity and build up the strength of your resilience muscle, predominantly by enduring a string of knock backs, put downs and screw ups!

And if you do feel like a failure, or an imposter as you read this, then you're in good company:

At thirty years old, one young dreamer was left devastated and depressed after being sacked from the company that he founded. That was Steve Jobs.

A few years back, a struggling rock and roll band were rejected by a string of recording studios and told they had no future. The band was the Beatles.

More recently, a young news presenter got demoted and told to give up television. You may have heard of her: Oprah Winfrey.

Then there's the guy who got fired from his job working for a newspaper, because he lacked imagination and original ideas. A young artist called Walt Disney. No wonder that he is quoted as saying, "courage is the main quality of leadership."

Another serial failure was an aspiring children's author. She got rejected not once, not twice, but twelve times by book publishers. Who would want to read a story about a wizard and his friends at school? JK Rowling went on to become the first billion dollar author. In her experience, "it is impossible to live without failing at something, unless you live so cautiously that you might as well not have lived at all."

And in the year 2000, with his credit cards maxed out, an up-and-coming community leader ran for congress, and lost. He failed spectacularly. This loser became the 44th president of the United States, Barack Obama.

What a bunch of failures.

And can you imagine what the world would have missed out on, if they had walked away and given up when they failed. But they had Heart. They refused to give up. They got knocked down. Then they got back up again. They kept the faith. And so their huge talent, contribution and ideas were not lost. They reached their dream destination.

The fact is all dream chasers suffer failures, disappointments and hardships. All pioneers bump up against resistance. And every dreamer will be rejected at some point. When you do fail (and you will) remind yourself why you got started. Dust yourself down and get back up to your feet. Don't lose faith. Keep trusting. Pray for the strength to try again.

Ultimately, failure is how you grow and mistakes are how you learn. Learn to embrace both and you will always get smarter, better and stronger. Dr Carol Dweck calls this the "Growth Mindset." You take the inner voice that says, "I can't do it" and you add a three letter word, "...*yet.*"

"I can't do it ..yet, I'll fail enough times until I can do it."

The comedian Jimmy Carr calls failure "a feedback loop," he says, "you should fail so many times that you run out of ways to fail and that's success."

Put simply, failure has a function: the same function pain serves in your body. The pain draws attention to the problem so you can fix it and learn from it. If you stub your toe on a chair, pretty soon you'll give that chair a wide berth as you walk by. If you keep failing at something, pretty soon, you'll notice what you're doing wrong and start getting it right.

When you're struggling, that's when you're stretching yourself, which means you're getting wiser and stronger. It's actually when you're under strain that you're growing.

Think about exercising a muscle. If you lift weights at a gym you strain a muscle until it is fatigued, effectively until that muscle "fails." Then, you go back a few days later and you find the same muscle is bigger and stronger, the cells have adapted to what you need them to do – to lift heavier things. Like a muscle being exercised to its failing point, so overcoming failures will make you stronger and more resilient. Similarly, learning from your mistakes will make you wiser. The goal is not to make the same mistake too many times in a row. Make new mistakes. This is also why, fundamentally, your past doesn't dictate your future. Your past mistakes aren't a precursor to future failure, they are just par for the course.

You're not giving up. You've just hit the wall. Like marathon runners who realise they still have a long way to go, and they feel they've nothing left to give; no reserves in the tank. They want to stop and sit down on the road. That's why friends and family line the route at the 18-20 mile point, to give a boost of encouragement and cheer the runner on when they need this the most.

For a leader, the wall is the moment when the toll and the huge cost of the journey seems too high a price to pay for the end destination. It might be fifty per cent or seventy five per cent into a project, but it happens to most leaders sooner or later.

The fact is, you've come too far to stop now; worked too hard to throw away all that effort you've put in. You've achieved so much, more than you thought you could, and you're so close now. When you make it past the wall, you'll be in the home straight, on your way to the finish line. Your dream is a marathon, not a sprint.

Remember, you don't have to be the fastest or the best, just be better than you were yesterday. Compete against yourself. And try not to have two bad days in a row. Progress can be slow, but you'll reach your dream destination if you don't stop.

Life doesn't get easier, but you do get better, smarter and stronger. Your Heart gets bigger.

And so, yesterday's seemingly insurmountable obstacle will soon be a tiny blip on the terrain below you, as you level up to new heights!

Good habits, repeated daily, weekly, monthly and yearly, combined with a healthy dose of determination and Heart will propel you further than you ever hoped or imagined. Successes don't come in giant leaps but in small steps.

Quite literally, we didn't get to the moon the day after JFK's famous speech on 12 September 1962. Human beings landed on the moon in 1969. It took 2,504 days of problem solving, getting up when the alarm goes off and working with teams who refused to give up, even when the task seemed impossible. It took six years and ten months of habits and heart; 60,096 hours of trial and error, mistakes and failure, struggling and resolving, to get the job done. And to make the moon dream history.

Habits and Heart are what it takes to see your dream become reality.

Habits and Heart are what it takes to stay on your Heading.

Habits and Heart are what makes someone a leader, when others give up and miss out.

All leaders endure hardship, face resistance and feel rejection. So, stay focussed, keep failing, and persevere. You will get there. You just haven't gotten there, yet.

If it was easy, everyone would do it. It's supposed to be difficult. Achieving anything that matters and changes things is difficult. But it's worth it, so do it anyway.

In the words of one dreamer, "We choose to go to the moon ... and do the other things, not because they're easy, but because they are hard."

Frequent Flyer

- Progress requires disciplined Habits. Keep doing the basics, over and over.

- Like a plane building up speed on a runway, progress is slow at first. Nothing happens, until everything happens.

- Our lives are the sum total of how we decide to spend our time.

- Calm yourself with B.L.E.S.T: Breath, Laugh, Exercise and Eat properly, Sleep well and Turn Off triggers.

- Show some mettle, some determination and some Heart.

- Mistakes are how you learn. Failure is how you grow. Learn to embrace both.

- Achieving anything that matters and changes things is difficult. Do it anyway.

"A goal gets us motivated, while a good habit keeps us motivated."
Aristotle

THE PLANE PARABLE

DARREN RICHARDS

PART 2

"ROLL"

LEADING OTHERS

As a leader, you have the antidote to fear and the solution to every crisis: it's called "faith."

Chapter 5
PASSENGER CABIN: HOPE
The Power of Story

On 1 June 2009, a state-of-the-art commercial airliner vanished from the air traffic radar screen. There was no mayday signal and the plane was brand new, just a few years old.

So, why did it fall out of the sky, so suddenly and inexplicably?

In the early hours of the morning, the airliner flew into a thunderstorm. After a short time, the autopilot switched off due to some strange airspeed readings.

With alarms blaring and multiple warnings illuminated, the on-duty pilot took manual control of the aircraft. With his instruments giving confusing readings, the pilot's attention turned to one problem he knew he *could* fix: the wings were not level.

Turbulence had caused the aircraft to "roll" slightly to the right, so he pushed the "side-stick" over to the left. Sadly, he overcompensated, rolling the wings the other way. For 30 long seconds, the plane lurched back and forth, rolling left and right, until the pilot succeeded and levelled out the wings.

But now the Airbus A330 was climbing too steeply and flying too high. As the pilot struggled to stop the roll, he had also pulled back on the stick, raising the nose and sending the passenger jet soaring three thousand feet above its cruising altitude. Even with the engines throttled up to maximum power, the angle of attack was just too acute for the wings to provide lift.

From the earliest aviators, like Wilbur and Orville, to modern trainee pilots, one fundamental principle becomes as instinctive as breathing. It's summed up by the well-worn phrase "pitch plus power equals performance."

In other words, if you put the horizon back in the window and put the throttle in the right notch for that kind of plane, you'll keep flying straight. So, when pilots want to prevent their engines cutting out, known as "stalling," they lower the nose of the aircraft, set the power to the right level and let air flow over the wings.

Tragically, the on-duty pilot of Air France 447 did the opposite.

Despite alarms ringing, warning the engines could stall, he kept raising the nose, pulling back and powering up. Another flight crew member rushed into the cockpit and asked to take control, but the on-duty pilot kept on pulling back on the main stick, overriding his efforts.

The plane hit the water at 2:14am, and sadly every soul was lost: 216 passengers and 12 crew, including the three highly capable commercial pilots.

Later an investigation would find that the autopilot disengaged because some of the heated airspeed sensors briefly clogged up with ice crystals. Heartbreakingly, this technical problem lasted a very short time, and the disaster could have been averted.

In the midst of a heavy thunderstorm, bombarded by alarms and not knowing which instruments could be trusted, the skilled pilot focussed on getting the wings level. In doing so, he lost sight of the basic laws of flight. This phenomenon is known as, "Cognitive Tunnelling". It occurs when we're jolted from a relaxed state to a sudden state of panic. Our heightened senses lock on to one glaring problem.

The autopilot had been active for four hours, when the pilot was abruptly forced to take control and he couldn't rely on his cockpit readings. The sudden stress and malfunctions caused him to lose his ability to focus on what mattered most. Instead, he zoned in on something he could fix, entering a "cognitive tunnel." This mental tunnel-vision meant he wasn't able to process more pressing dangers or take in critical information, like his altitude and the dangerously steep angle of the plane. The pilot lost sight of the bigger picture.

As human beings, every one of us is susceptible to the horrible sensation of panic. Leaders, especially, are faced with surprise stress, unprecedented pressures and unforeseen events that strike out of the blue. These challenges and problems are figurative flashing lights that ring alarm bells for us. They jolt us into urgent action, just when we thought everything was going so smoothly.

When crisis comes to visit, it doesn't knock gently when you're rested and ready; it's more like a brick that smashes through your front window in the middle of the night, making your heart race and your head a foggy mess.

You can never predict what crisis you'll face, or when that brick will crash in on you, but you can prepare for a crisis; knowing full well one will turn up uninvited soon enough. Far better to *expect* and prepare for a crisis now, before the crisis inevitably reveals itself and demands a cool-headed response (usually when you're least able to muster one).

When a crisis hits you, the first thing to do is *nothing whatsoever*. Just stop. Don't act before you've had a chance to learn and then to think. Don't misdiagnose the problem or enter a cognitive tunnel, by fixating on the first glaring symptom you recognise.

Instead, start by steadying yourself. Just pause and take a long slow breath, or three. Step back from the noise and any conflicting read outs. If you can, physically withdraw to a quieter place; go into another room and close the door. Raise your head from the flashing lights and information overload and take a moment to look out the window. This will help you to see the whole picture: your plane is still in the air, you're not about to crash. If you have time, use the full spectrum of B.L.E.S.T. steps to think more clearly and regain a sense of perspective.

Next, gather as many reliable and verifiable facts as you can. Find out what's actually going on. Assess the situation. Reflect on the possible implications. Don't get focused on one missing piece of the puzzle. Just do your best and accept that some things will not be knowable. Ask advice from a few wise heads and consider your options.

Finally, make an orderly plan to tackle the crisis. What needs to be done urgently, and what can wait? Do as much as you need to, to resolve the imminent threat or danger and create a timeline for the rest. Remember, how others see you respond, is as important as what you actually decide to do or say.

Fear is Contagious but so is Calm

"The best piece of advice I ever got in Navy Seal training is simple: Calm is contagious."
Rorke Denver

As a leader, most of the challenges you face won't come as a minute of mayhem – they'll feel more like a marathon of misgivings, mistakes and misunderstandings.

Everything can be going smoothly when suddenly you fly into a storm: something shifts and makes the journey to your dream destination a lot more unsettling for your passengers.

Perhaps you experience a change in your team, your finances, your health or your environment. These storms can happen on a big scale, affecting a whole country or a group of nations or on a small scale, affecting just your own project, your team or your friends and family. After the highs and excitement of the lift-off phase and some early wins together, when setbacks and disappointment do happen, passengers naturally begin to worry and complain. Whether it's a sudden crisis, a stressful conflict or simply the need for change, it will have an impact on your people. Sometimes this means the people journeying with you will start to grumble or display doubts about the destination.

As social animals, anxiety and unease can quickly grow into group panic. Left unchecked, fear is highly contagious. In stormy situations, fear is like a virus that spreads panic from one person to the next. The psychological term is called "Social Proof," coined by Robert Cialdini. It says we copy other people's actions in order to fit in and conform to the norms of our community. In short, if one person panics, you can expect it will soon be "caught" by others, who will then proceed to follow that lead unconsciously and instinctively.

Unfortunately, fear will often *look like* anger. And panic can present as painful remarks, usually aimed at the leader. The fight-or-flight response makes people act impulsively, not rationally. So, they may well say things that are completely out of character, then feel regret once they've calmed down.

As a leader, social proof will be a headwind that blows against you, but you can also turn it to your advantage. You can make it a tailwind to propel you. Your unfaltering belief in the destination can be the vaccine that subdues the panic virus.

If a plane is bouncing around, but the airline staff are smiling and calm, the passengers feel reassured. In the same way, your followers will look to you, to see how you're responding.

When everything seems to be going wrong, you may be tempted to give up or to doubt yourself. Personally, you may feel scared. You may even feel like you want to run and hide from your critics and your problems, but this is a critical time. The very best thing you can do is to communicate your belief that everything will be okay and to impart a reassuring tone.

You can be honest and say you share their disappointment, concerns or sadness, whilst conveying your unshakable faith that it will all be worth it when you finally "arrive." This will help to restore calm for your passengers. When faced with doubts, insults, accusations or backbiting, a leader's emotional composure is what keeps the plane on the right heading.

Don't lose your temper. Maintain your belief in the dream and keep your cool. Aim to communicate gently and to reassure sensitively, conveying positivity and inspiring optimism.

As a leader, you have the antidote to fear and the solution to every crisis: it's called "faith." A leader's faith in the destination will cultivate calm in their followers or team. You can help your team to stop and look out the window to see that you're still flying steady and straight. Especially when you notice people entering the "Cognitive Tunnel," you can help them find their way out.

Always remember, fear is contagious, but so is calm. You will convey feelings of safety and peacefulness, simply by modelling and communicating the same. You can douse the flames of fear, quenching them with your faith.

When George W. Bush received the dreadful news that a second plane had crashed into the World Trade Centre, he knew this meant the USA was under attack. Rather than jump up and react, he made the conscious decision to stay and listen to a school child read aloud.

In his words, *"Leaders set the tone for crisis, and so I made the decision to stay seated and wait for an appropriate moment to leave rather than scare the children."*

> *"Leadership is the ability to hide your panic from others."*
> **Lao Tzu**

Fear is the human default mode; it's our autopilot. Panic is hardwired into people. As a leader you are not immune from this. When we're suddenly faced with a threat or pressure, it's natural to feel overwhelmed and scared at first. Especially when we're lacking a good night's sleep or stretching ourselves in some way. The "fuel" of our inner personal resources can run low. Remember, where fear *reacts*; faith waits, faith trusts, and faith *responds* calmly and confidently.

What about when we find our own faith well drying up? This is often because we've stopped trusting. We stopped trusting God, we stopped trusting others, or we've stopped trusting in our own ability to make good decisions. Left unchecked, fear will make you feel weak, indecisive, distracted and even unwell. But faith and trust will make you strong again.

Nevertheless, even when you feel weak or ill-equipped, sometimes you still have to smile and hide your own fears as a leader, so that others can draw strength from you, keep believing and keep going; to care enough to not show you're scared.

Anyone can be pessimistic and fearful. Anyone can panic. Instead, choose to keep the faith. Choose to remain enthusiastic and optimistic about the destination. This will draw others to you. Unshakable faith is an uncommon, attractive and valuable thing to have and to share with those you lead.

"Cool, calm and composed" is always the right response to a crisis. Staying calm is like having a superpower. It always gets you halfway towards solving a problem.

Refuse to let fear push you around. Instead, learn to "greet the fear" like an expected visitor, then show it the door. Take a deep breath, exhale slowly and pray for peace, discernment and wisdom. In this way, you may avoid entering your own "cognitive tunnel." Take a look up at the horizon and remind yourself you're still alive and still flying. Then gather a few wise advisors and make a plan to solve the problem or end the crisis. You may have to re-route the autopilot, but always keep the coordinates of your dream destination locked in.

So, be that rare person who can keep their head (and their heading) when all around are losing theirs, to paraphrase Rudyard Kipling. Stay calm, re-group and if need be, alter your route, but never change your destination.

Stories have the power to En-Courage

"Do not let any unwholesome talk come out of your mouths, but only what is helpful for building others up according to their needs, that it may benefit those who listen."
Ephesians 4:29

Be an encourager.

Encouragement is so rare these days – that just wielding a specific word of praise can create an incredible impact in someone's life. Encouragement actually builds a person up. It's more than words, it's a mechanism and lever lifting someone, empowering them to aim for and achieve more than they could before you spoke. We're not robots. Our brains respond to others' belief in us.

When you say, "Since you joined the team, I've really noticed you're just brilliant at..." and single out something specific about their character or skills, I guarantee they'll keep doing that thing and even strive to get better at it, from that moment on.

You see, the word "encourage" is derived from an Old French word, "encoragier," which means "to make strong, or hearten."

That first part "en" means to "put in" or to "make." So, when we en-courage someone, we "put strength in their heart." What a thing to be able to do! You can actually place more courage and strength into the heart of someone else.

So how else can you share some of your "courage" with others? With a story.

When we tell hope-filled stories, we "put courage" into the heart of our hearers. Call it a "hopeful-heart transplant." Telling stories places courage and hope in your team, audience or community, when setbacks, slumps and disappointments inevitably come.

This is why all dreamers should be storytellers. Learn to tell your story and the stories of the people you care about, to give others strength to keep them going on the journey towards your dream destination.

In short, tell stories of hope, about where you are headed. This is why, Hope tells stories in the Plane Parable: to remind, envision and encourage the passengers.

Hope's happy stories remind the people why the bumpy journey is worth it: to reach their shared dream destination, painting a vivid picture of the destination to inspire afresh. And her stories re-envision the passengers, they encourage and invoke optimism from one heart and mind to another.

Hope is so crucial. But when panic and doubt are allowed to get fully grown, they can cause a crippling feeling of hopelessness. According to the dictionary definition, "an individual who feels hopeless may often have no expectation of future improvement or success." The Bible even goes so far as to say, "hope deferred makes the heart grow *sick*." When people genuinely lose hope they stop believing that a better future is possible, which makes them miserable and even ill. Hopelessness is dangerous, even deadly.

This is why "Hope" is positioned at the very centre of the plane diagram. It's a universal human need that lays at the heart of every dream and team.

Not an "empty hope" that something good "might" happen, but a sure and steady belief that the dream "will happen" one day; an assured and trusting faith that "all will be well." Hope will steady and sustain you when the storm is raging and the threats that surround are genuinely formidable. And hope will give people courage and strength to carry on, to persevere, and to take the right risks.

Hope, like courage, can be given like a gift to other people, through story.

Stories of Hope have the power to change people

Seasoned storyteller, Rob Parsons, observes that, "stories are older than fire." This is why stories hold such power to change how people feel, think and act.

From cave dwelling primeval hand-painters to ornate and colourful mediaeval tapestries, human beings have always been storytellers. Our first language as a species is allegory, metaphor and visual narratives.

"The greatest thing by far is to be a master of metaphor; it is the one thing that cannot be learnt from others; and it is also a sign of genius."
Aristotle

There's a reason why this book is based on a simple story about a plane. You will remember this plane and some of what happens in the parable long after you forget what follows in the later chapters. This is because people retain forty per cent more information when it's presented as a story.

Perhaps this is why Jesus told parables that often contained metaphors, such as building a house on sand or rock, finding a pearl of great value, or comparing God's Word to seed falling on different types of soil.

It's why Dr King's dream speech packed such an emotional punch, since he was a master of metaphor and could paint powerful word-pictures. He described images you can't help but visualise in your mind's eye, carefully crafting objects and metaphors with evocative layers of meaning. For example, "we will ...hew out of the mountain of despair a stone of hope... transform the jangling discords of our nation into a beautiful symphony of brotherhood."

Metaphors always make your message more memorable and persuasive. When you use a metaphor or an allegory, you're asking your hearers to meet you halfway. You offer a line drawing and they add the colour and figure out the meaning for themselves. They personalise the image you offer and place themselves at its heart.

Before literacy was even widespread, and even before books were widely available, stories were a reliable way for whole civilisations to pass knowledge down to the next generation, to safeguard culture and instil good values. This is called the Oral Tradition. In fact, humans have been verbal storytellers far longer than we've been writers and readers.

For thousands of years, stories have also proven to be a powerful tool for persuasion. They enable the storyteller to spark a rapid emotional connection and cause their hearers to literally "feel" positivity predisposed towards the communicator and their subject matter.

Our brains are wired to convert stories into emotions, from the earliest civilisations telling tales huddled around smouldering fires, eating meals together and retelling familiar fables to bind families and bond communities, to the modern epic sagas, like *Star Wars*, *The Avengers* and *Lord of the Rings*. We love legends and we adore sharing in the emotional highs and lows of beloved heroes as they overcome the odds to save populations in peril.

Stories of Hope have the power to persuade and to change someone's emotional response.

When you tell a story, the brain of your hearer actually "syncs up" with your own. Researchers who used an FMRI machine to monitor the brains of storytellers and of their hearers discovered that the same parts of the brain were activated in the hearer, leading them to feel a sense of agreement and rapport with the storyteller.

Other studies have evidenced the power of a "story of hope" to influence people's brains, and they were able to measure the effect on hearers' hormone levels.

Dr Paul Zak found that character-led stories with a dramatic narrative arc – where the main protagonist overcomes adversity and wins the day – actively triggers the release of Oxytocin in the hearer. This goes some way to explain how watching a play or seeing a movie at the cinema can totally change how we feel, by the time we leave the theatre.

By taking blood samples before and after an "overcomer" story, Dr Zak found Oxytocin levels were measurably raised. Oxytocin motivates people to behave in more altruistic, caring, cooperative ways. The hormone is usually synthesised in our bodies when we feel that someone trusts us or when we are the recipient of an act of kindness. Oxytocin is a feel-good hormone that helps us feel a strong emotional bond to another person. It boosts our feelings of empathy and affinity as well as our propensity for being generous. Oxytocin levels are, therefore, a reliable indicator for how much money someone will donate to charity.

When you tell a story people begin to relax and to physically feel better, they allow people to empathise emotionally with a person, need or important cause you are putting before them.

Stories also help your hearers to trust you, even when they've never met you before. Tell a personal human story, with a powerful emotive arc about an overcomer, and your hearer will begin to form an emotional connection with you. They'll also find it easier to recall what you'd said about the project or cause you're presenting.

When I speak to groups, no matter how long I have to speak, I always open with a personal story with appropriate vulnerability. I also try to inject some humour if the setting allows. I will tell an anecdote about my family or a quirky situation that makes people smile at first, and then drop into content that's more moving or sad, to create an emotional juxtaposition.

Whenever you share your dream, always wrap it in a powerful personal story. Lead with a little vulnerability and talk about someone who has overcome adversity, don't just reel off statistics and show facts on a PowerPoint slide. Show your audience how the vision changes lives. By opening up and sharing something about yourself, you can demonstrate that you trust an audience, which usually causes this release of Oxytocin, increasing empathy and compassion. It makes your hearer more amenable to an opportunity to make a difference. They will be more likely to agree to your invitation to help change lives.

As a leader, your storytelling will attract new people, and draw others who share your vision, values and hopes for the future. Tell stories that paint a visual picture of your preferred future when you cast your vision. This may be your origin story, where you talk about your own journey to launching a project or idea or it might be a story about someone you're trying to help, and the challenges they face every day.

If possible, use visual aids; not just slides, but a physical object you can hold in your hand. If you must use a slide, then show a photo of the person you're telling the story about and let their photo take up a whole screen.

Find new ways to make your message more memorable and to bring it to life for your hearer. Help them form a clear picture of who you're speaking about and how their life will be changed. Sync the picture in their mind with the future vision in your mind. As a fundraiser, I always tell stories about individuals that the charity is helping. I ensure we have permission first, which is paramount, and I only use their first name, not their surname. I also hold up simple objects to make my talks more memorable, such as a handheld mirror, a climbing rope, or a pebble painted with a floral pattern. Anything that will bring the metaphor to life and cement the image in my hearer's mind. If you ask someone what I said, a few hours later, they'll always talk about the visual aid object, and this will jog their memory about the meaning behind it.

Slides are fine, but they lose their impact when you clog them with alarming statistics and pie charts. The truth is, people make decisions with their hearts, based on emotion, and then they justify these decisions later, with their heads, using logic and reason. Appeal to the heart first, but don't neglect the head. This is what lies behind Aristotle's well-known triad of Pathos (emotion and appealing to the heart), Ethos (establishing your credibility and credentials), and Logos (using logic and appealing to the head, with facts, stats and academic reasoning).

"New Customers Only"

Does it bother you, when a company offers a fantastic deal for new customers only, but when you come to buy again or renew – as a long standing and loyal customer – you're refused the same deal?

The same mistake can be made by leaders.

They tell their stories and cast their vision to new people but forget to retell the stories of hope to their long-standing team, followers and supporters. They assume "I told them already — I don't want to repeat myself and bore them. Plus, they know why this matters by now."

It's not just the newbies who need to hear your stories. You have to remind your team and your loyal supporters and partners on a regular basis. When you pour vision into people, you'll find that they leak! So, keep topping them up.

Sometimes, when the journey has been long and arduous, people just forget why they joined in the first place. They forget, but they also begin to doubt and worry. Will the destination you've described really be worth it? Is it too good to be true? Can they trust you to reach the goal safely?

You can and must raise hope, courage and strength in those who follow you, when fears and fatigue set in, slumps and disappointments happen and when the initial launch excitement dissipates into discipline and hard work.

Help them to remember why they signed up in the first place and why they initially decided to get "onboard," before the flight got "bumpy." Re-paint your visual picture of the dream destination, over and over again. Until you're bored of saying it. When you're sick of saying the same story and spelling out the dream and why it matters, that's when others may just be starting to get it. I guarantee it takes longer than you think for vision to stick. So, keep telling stories of hope about the future. Help your team to recapture the dream destination in their own mind's eye. And use metaphors and words you could also draw, since these are words that people can also imagine. "Crusty bread rolls and steaming hot tomato soup" is far better than using the word "lunch"; you can picture the rolls and hot soup and almost taste them. So, tell stories about the people who will be helped and choose words that people can picture.

Whether you're addressing your old faithful troops or brand new recruits, as we see from the studies, your stories of hope will literally alter people's emotions: from fear to courage, and from frustration to inspiration. You can lift people up and energise your audience with stories that move them emotionally and move them into action.

Stories come into their own most of all when your team are suffering from *internal* fears, frustrations and doubts or from *external* setbacks and discouragements. When times get tough (and they will) always use a story to reframe the adversity and find the opportunity in the midst of the challenge. Michael Caine calls this technique, "using the difficulty."

Take a lack of funding; some leaders then begin to spiral into negative and fearful narratives, for instance: *"It's not looking good. I'm feeling the pressure now. If we don't raise £10,000, we'll be forced to close the project down. You have to try harder!"*

This approach doesn't encourage or instil hope. Instead, the same challenge can be turned into an opportunity, using a story of hope: *"No doubt about it, we're in a tough spot. But we haven't come all this way to quit now. Just think about children like David. His powered wheelchair needs a new battery pack. Or Jenny, who's going without breakfast so she can feed her kids before school. They're counting on us, and we're going to come through for them. What we need now is 100 kind people to donate £100. Any ideas how we can get the word out?"*

The problem is the same, but it's framed differently. The first version is filled with panic, guilt and fear. The second uses a story to remind the partners why the dream matters and assumes a solution is just around the corner, making it seem manageable and realistic.

How to tell your Story of Hope

I've developed a structure for telling stories and asking people to partner with a project or cause: C-F-R-O-G-S, so you don't get a "frog" in your throat when it comes to sharing your dream!

This model provides a powerful narrative arc, with a central character who overcomes adversity. It also helps ensure a strong opening and ending, with a clear "call to action."

It answers some key questions in your hearer's mind:

Curiosity	- Why should I listen to you?
Family	- Do I trust you?
Reason	- What problem are you inviting me to help solve?
One Changed Life	- Why should I care?
Goal	- How can this problem be solved?
So What?	- What do you want me to do about it?

Before you speak, write some notes and prepare well. Rehearse what you want to say, until you know it by heart or as close as you can get.

As you get up to speak, take a long, slow, calm, deep breath in. Then SMILE and make eye contact with a few people around the room.

Finally, work through your story structure:

Curiosity – Why should I listen to you?

Grab people's attention right at the start with a mysterious statement or an intriguing question. Spark their curiosity and make them want to listen.

For example:

> *I just found out something incredible, and I want to share it with you.*

> *Can I start with a confession?*

> *Have you ever wondered why...?*

> *Isn't it funny how...?*

Followed by,

> *Hi, my name is _____ from _____.*

Family – Do I trust you?

Once you have people's attention, pivot quickly to a *true* story as fast as you can. Link the opening statement to a trust-building anecdote. Perhaps use an amusing moment from family life with the full prior permission of those you mention. And never lie – it damages your credibility. Aim for endearing and trustworthy, not superior or boastful.

Use dialogue, quoting a timeframe and location.

Use words they could draw.

Use a simple and relevant visual aid.

Give people hope. Don't depress them.

You can also use this anecdote and your visual aid to introduce a theme, such as "seeing yourself differently" (holding a mirror) or "suddenly I could see a way forward" (perhaps, turning on a torch).

Reason – What problem are you inviting me to help solve?

Find a natural link from your own light-hearted story to the one big problem you're looking to help solve, and back it up with one powerful fact or jarring statistic.

For example:

But at least we have food on our plate. It's shocking to me that fifteen per cent of all...

But I never had to worry whether I'd make it home safely, like one in ten of...

Thankfully, I had a hot plate of chips waiting for me at home. But over 250 people will sleep rough tonight on the freezing streets of our city.

One Changed Life – Why should I care?

Tell the story of one real person that your project or idea will help. "Funnel down" from the abstract statistic to a real life that needs help. Use their first name (with permission) to put a human face on the problem. Again, use words you could draw, to help your audience to picture the adversity or injustice this person faces.

Goal – How can this problem be solved?

Tell people what you want to do about this problem. Keep it simple – don't reel off a long list. Stay high level. What's your one big ambitious goal, in a nutshell, that could help the person you just described, and others like them? This should be inspiring.

For example:

We exist to give every person like John the chance to start afresh.

We passionately believe that Jenny and others like her should eat three square meals a day.

We are determined to provide fully stocked fridges for more people like Jacky.

So What? – What do you want me to do about it?

Finally, be clear about how you want people to respond. You've taken them on a journey, now spell out the part you'd like them to play. What opportunity are you offering, for them to be a part of this amazing solution?

"So, today, I'm here to ask you, please will you **[action]**, and together we will **[link back to the visual aid and theme]**."

For example:

So, today, please will you give a financial gift and together we'll light the way forward for more people, like John.

So, today, I'm here to ask you, please will you pray for our team and together we'll help people like Jenny to see themselves differently.

So, today, I'm here to ask you, please will you join our volunteer team and together we'll give people like Jacky fresh food and, more importantly, fresh hope.

Some final tips:

- Aim to speak for between ten and twenty minutes.

- Speak slower than you think you should.

- Allow pauses for emphasis, on the key points.

- Don't hide behind a lectern or music stand.

- Instead of thinking "I feel nervous," try thinking "I feel excited."

- Just be yourself – don't try and copy the best speaker or comedian you've heard.

Your stories of hope will naturally inspire others, offering a clear picture of your dream destination and placing faith and courage into their hearts.

Remember, stories move people, stories *en*-courage and stories persuade.

Frequent Flyer

- Storms make the journey bumpy, so people start to worry, complain and criticise.

- Fear is contagious, but so is calm.

- A leader's emotional composure and unswerving belief in the destination can calm people's fears. It will restore people's faith and peace.

- Stories of Hope envision people; reminding them why they joined in the first place.

- Tell your own story to build connection and trust.

- Stories of Hope change emotions: from fear to courage and from anger to inspiration.

- Use C-F-R-O-G-S to structure your stories and communicate your dream – aim for the heart, not just the head.

"We must neither be cowardly, nor rash,
but courageous."
Aristotle

THE PLANE PARABLE

People are generally better persuaded by the reasons which they have themselves discovered than by those which have come into the mind of others.

Chapter 6
WINGS: HEARD & HELD
The virtue between two extremes

"Leadership is influence, nothing more, nothing less.
And leadership is a behaviour you can learn."
Rev. Celia Apeagyei-Collins

Fusaichi Pegasus was once bought for seventy million dollars. It's not a gemstone or a private jet, but a *racehorse,* named after the winged steed in Greek mythology who threw off his rider and then flew up into the night sky. Gaze at the heavens tonight and you may well see the Pegasus star constellation, resembling the front half of a galloping horse.

Horses were clearly important to the ancient Greeks, who could take an unpredictable and powerful animal and train it to stay calm amidst the melee of battle. They could tame a wild horse and make it "meek," harnessing its power for a purpose.

"Meekness" isn't something you hear about very often. It's derived from the ancient Greek word "praus," meaning "strong and subdued." Far from implying "weakness," "meekness" encapsulates being very powerful whilst possessing another, rarer strength: the toughness and discipline to keep this power contained so it can be harnessed and channelled. An aircraft jet engine could be considered "meek," as gallons of explosive propellant are harnessed safely to provide intricate variations of thrust and power. A jet aircraft can speed up or slow down at the will of a pilot who is able to restrain and regulate the immense power at his fingertips.

To be "meek" is to exert power under control. To be strong but remain self-controlled, at the same time. Aristotle called it *"the virtue ...between two extremes."* And the same term is used by Jesus, "Blessed are the *meek*, for they shall inherit the earth." (Matthew 5:5).

Few people are able to remain composed and retain their resolve. Meekness is a high wire balancing act, performed above the circus of distractions, disagreements and detractors. Master meekness and you may well "inherit the earth."

Meek Amid the Melee

Eventually, leading others will bring you to some turbulent times. You'll be buffeted by headwinds and forces outside of your control. These seasons of challenge are not much fun when you're travelling through them, but when you look back you'll find they are often the formative experiences that strengthened your relationships and drew you closer to your team. How you lead through the melee and mess of life is what makes you worthy of followers; it can often earn you their trust, gratitude and loyalty longer-term.

When you've been moving towards your destination for a while, your passengers can become restless and will begin asking questions of you and the route you've chosen. At other times, when they're feeling discomfort or pain of various kinds, they'll look to you to solve their problems and make everything okay.

Either way, when the people you lead begin to complain or even criticise you, you may be tempted to "change course" in the hope of a smoother ride. Resist this temptation. The common mistake many new leaders make is to doubt themselves. They try to placate and please the people they're tasked with leading. In an effort to keep people happy, you stop leading and start allowing followers to dictate the destination. Seasoned leaders, with more experience, know that dream destinations are always found on the other side of some turbulent skies.

After an initial honeymoon period, problems and gripes tend to build up. When this happens the people who follow you will naturally look to you for answers and solutions. They will want you to fix their frustrations. They will want to know when the difficulties will end and how you're going to solve the problems.

You can't possibly be responsible for solving every problem, meeting every need and rectifying every wrong. You're not the all-powerful Wizard of Oz. You have a finite amount of time, energy and capacity. You'll only end up exhausted if you try to figure out every answer on your own. You may even make yourself unwell, which means you won't be able to reach your dream destination or help others reach theirs either.

The trick is to be "meek" during turbulent times, turning adversity to your advantage.

And step one is: don't get in a F.L.A.P.

New leaders fall into a "FLAP" when the ride gets bumpy. In other words, they reveal a: *"Fear of Leading Angry People."*

The people you lead will most likely get angry or become more critical of you when *nothing* much is happening. They can grow impatient and begin to doubt your leadership. Likewise, they can become more vocal when *everything* seems to be happening (they have too much to deal with) when the skies become rough and they are jolted about, figuratively speaking.

You may dislike conflict. Most people do. This is perfectly natural and normal. However, when others do get angry or complain in times of turbulence, leaders should avoid three common pitfalls: *self-pity*, *capitulation* and *strong-arming*.

Self-Pity

You could be forgiven for feeling a bit sorry for yourself. You're working long hours and perhaps even neglecting your own needs, so you expect people would notice and be more grateful. It's not easy being a leader and being responsible for others, and so your first reaction might be self-pity. Then, if others remain unsympathetic, your emotions may quickly turn to resentment or frustration with the people you're leading. From the perspective of your followers, this will make you appear unapproachable, uncaring and even arrogant. Self-pity, especially angry self-pity, will always make the situation worse, for you and for them.

When we're criticised, attacked or mocked, whether to our face or behind our back, our instinctive inclination is to defend ourselves. When someone hurts you with their words or actions, our natural instinct is to say hurtful things in reply; to blame the person and point out their faults and flaws. But as we talked about in the Habits chapter, recognising when our brain is entering "Flight Mode" is crucial here. If someone makes you feel incompetent, small or disrespected, take a moment to scan your emotions and the physical reaction in your body. The chances are, you're going to be angry, which shuts down the rational part of your brain and causes you to make bad decisions. To react without any regard for the consequences.

When you hit a patch of turbulence and those you're leading seem ungrateful — when they begin to blame and berate you — never lose your temper. Don't get angry. When you lose your temper, you've lost the argument and you've lost control of the situation.

As it says in Proverbs 20:3, "Every fool is quick to quarrel."

If you feel angry with people you're leading, recognise this and work through the BLEST steps. You'll then be more able to respond wisely rather than reacting angrily.

Instead, "treat others as you'd like to be treated." Choose to speak well of others, both to their face and behind their back. Refuse to criticise back, even if they criticise you. Think back: when has a criticism ever resulted in another person changing their position, backing down or doing what you want? It doesn't work. They're more likely to double-down. What's more, you never look good trying to make someone else look bad.

Experienced leaders learn its best not to retaliate and instead to fly at a higher attitude: to "rise above" unkind insults, draining skirmishes and baseless accusations. They never allow others to knock them off course or distract them from their goal – the dream destination.

Ultimately, you'll be judged by *where you land* and w*ho you took with you.* Let this speak for you. Don't be easily provoked or offended. Just let your dream do the talking.

The Capitulation-Domination Pendulum

Another instinctive response to unhappy followers is "apologetic capitulation." You keep saying "sorry" and asking your team or followers what you should do instead of what you had decided upon. On the surface this may seem empowering, but it's perceived as you being weak and incompetent. Who wants to follow a leader who is not certain about where they're actually going, or how to take others there safely? Imagine setting off on a long journey in a foreign land and your guide turning around to ask you for directions!

Many inexperienced leaders fall into the trap of thinking their role is to keep everyone happy and everything harmonious. In turbulent times this drives new leaders to one of two extremes: either they become too harsh and domineering (bulldozing and strong-arming anyone who disagrees with them using fear, demoralisation and intimidation tactics) or they swing to the other side of the pendulum (they panic, crumble and capitulate). They have a crisis of confidence – in themselves and their dream. This is when they turn around to ask their followers for "directions," in an attempt to make everyone happy again. It's not uncommon to get caught in this pattern of hearing a complaint, doubting yourself, then blindly enacting whatever alternative is put forward, even when you know it will move everyone further away from their dream destination.

When leaders behave like this, they end up having to do a "U-turn" on a lot of decisions. Especially if more vocal or rival team members make contradictory demands (that's when chaos ensues). It's like prising open a brass compass casing then forcing the needle to point in the direction of the prevailing wind! If you lead like this you'll never end up where you've set out to go.

Ultimately, neither side of the pendulum – domination *or* capitulation – work for long. Both scare people away to a safer captain and calmer seas. If you can't lead them somewhere good, they'll look elsewhere.

So, if strong-arming doesn't work and appeasing makes things worse, what is the answer?

Be Kind AND Strong

"One of the criticisms I've faced over the years is that I'm not aggressive enough... somehow because I'm empathetic, it must mean I'm weak. I totally rebel against that.

I refuse to believe that you cannot be both compassionate and strong."

Jacinda Ardern, *former Prime Minister of New Zealand.*

Some dreamers are too strong and harsh, tramping over people to reach their destination, no matter the cost. Others are too weak and indecisive, bowing to pressure and fearing angry followers. Yet, you can strike a balance, being compassionate *and yet* strong; caring *and still* decisive, at the same time. You can be "meek."

The key is to provide *high levels of support* and in doing so you are afforded permission to offer *high levels of challenge*.

High levels of challenge are only possible when followers feel safe, trusted and cared for, when they trust your motives and when they've confidence in your ability to lead.

Most of us want to be liked, we want to be popular, naturally. But leaders just can't be popular all the time. Truth be told, you can't always be best friends with those you lead, as eventually you'll have to take decisions that may make you unpopular. In the words of a former UK Prime Minister Tony Blair, "when you decide, you divide."

Staying strong means not backing down in order to be liked. It requires some mental toughness to make tough calls if you really do want everyone to arrive safely at your dream destination. But being strong also means *staying kind* and being caring too, even as you make those tough calls and judgements. This takes huge courage; it takes Heart. This is the essence of "Meek" leadership: finding a sweet spot between autonomy *and* accountability, individual ownership *and* collective collaboration, human kindness *and* an honest appraisal of performance. A balance has to be discerned between the needs and feelings of *the individual* and the hopes of *the team,* in order to achieve mutual *objectives*. Meek leaders combine reassuringly competent, calm decision-making with caring consultation and empowering high-trust collaboration.

The bottom line is to never lower your standards just to keep people happy. If what you're doing really matters, then your primary beneficiaries deserve nothing less than your best. Ultimately, the standard you'll accept is the standard you'll get. So, treat people with dignity, respect and kindness, but also expect high standards and real results for the people you're seeking to help.

"You don't inspire your teammates by showing them how amazing you are.

You inspire by showing them how amazing they are."
Robyn Benincasa, *World Champion Racer*

Leaders shouldn't be strong in a way that reminds others they're weak. Instead you need to be strong *for* the people you lead; a protective and nurturing strength; not the kind that uses force or evokes fear.

As the old adage goes, the sun and the wind were having a contest, to see who could force a man to remove his thick coat. The wind blew a mighty gale, but the man only clung to his coat more tightly. After a time, it was the sun's turn. The sun gently warmed the man until his face grew pink and sweat poured from his brow. Willingly, gladly and quickly, the man removed his coat and threw it to the ground giving out a sigh of relief. *The moral of the story is, the more you try to impose your will and control, the less you'll be heard!*

Always wield power you're entrusted with in a genuinely selfless way; use it to achieve the shared goal, helping others learn and grow as you move closer to the destination together. *How you journey*, and what people learn on the way, matters just as much as reaching the end point.

The kind of strength a leader needs then, is not that of a dictator or bully. Aggression, shouting and force have no place in modern leadership, outside of the armed forces. Even in the uniformed services orders are issued amidst a prevailing culture of teamwork, comradery, loyalty, service, duty and sacrifice.

Your strength can, and should, make other people feel stronger and more capable. Whereas those who use fear or "gas lighting," make their followers less effective, because they become more dependent and indecisive. When you challenge, you should always be motivated by wanting the best for the other person and for the shared project, never an overflow of anger or a way to hurt someone back.

So, never be unkind or intentionally malicious. Honour and care for people, but make sure your cause or goal always comes before personal preferences, including your own at times.

Soothe, Don't Solve

"People don't care what you know, until they know that you care.
Touch their heart, before asking for a hand."
Rev. Celia Apeagyei-Collins

The people you lead need you to be strong and positive *for them*. It's actually reassuring for those you're leading when you have certainty and conviction about the route and destination. Equally, your confidence and your competence can sooth people's panic and calm their fears. Sometimes all someone really needs to hear is, *"We will get through this. It's going to be okay,"* or *"You've got this. I'm behind you. I believe in you."*

Being *strong for others,* validates and confirms their decision to travel alongside you. Just as a jet engine contains the energy of burning fuel, a meek approach will contain people's fears and channel their creative faculties into finding a solution. You can show them how to learn from their failures and turn their frustration into the resolution for remedy.

When those around you lack the experience, knowledge or skills or when a situation feels overwhelming, you have the ability to impart certainty and clarity. Projecting calm into their crisis, you can then help a team member overcome self-doubt and instil galvanizing belief. People will start coming to you for help, and even respecting you more, when spending time with you reassures them and also reveals their potential to solve problems on their own. That's not to say that you alone will have the elusive answer to what ails them.

The best way to do this is with questions. Help the other person come to their own conclusion by asking questions that enable them to consider the various likely consequences of different courses of action.

Or, as kids would say: "Help me do it alone."

When you try and tell someone what to do, it will almost always make them want to do the exact opposite. Impose rules and you'll reap rebellion every time. Instead, they must discover things for themselves. As Blaise Pascal observed, "People are generally better persuaded by the reasons which they have themselves discovered than by those which have come into the mind of others."

Spelling out your solution is counterproductive, as people will never learn for next time. Plus, what once worked for you may not work for their scenario. People must generate, sift and settle on solutions for themselves.

So, try not to "write prescriptions," or your patient will come back later and say, "your solution didn't work, give me another prescription." Aim to be more of a coach than a doctor. Good leaders are similar to sports coaches: they're not there to hand out orders and pronounce their solution; they're more of a guide. Be someone they can run to on the edge of the field and safely say, "I'm struggling: can you help me find a way through?" Choose to be the kind of leader who sends players back out onto the field with more confidence, sharpened skills and a better chance of success. It may be a cliché, but when your team succeeds, you succeed.

The only reliable way to influence someone is to listen to them: to discover the need from their point of view and then help them find their own way through. Leaders should become adept in the skill of hearing and understanding another person's experience and perspective. What are they worried about? What do they hope for? What matters to them? Consider their needs, before you ask them to do something for you.

The Four Needs of Followers

A "Meek" leader understands that followers have four principal needs. When you meet these four primary needs, you can earn their loyalty and the opportunity to ask for help:

1. To feel TRUSTED   (be empowering and high trust)

2. To feel HOPE   (be an optimist, expect the best)

3. To feel HEARD   (be a caring and kind listener)

4. To feel HELD   (be confident and decisive)

Let's unpack each need.

"I feel trusted"

Trust is key to unlocking any dream, as we discussed earlier. And trust lies at the heart of every healthy relationship, team and dream. When others feel like you trust them, that you assume the best of them and have high expectations of them, they'll believe in themselves more.

Trust "looks like" giving people an appropriate level of autonomy to take decisions and even to make mistakes: so they can fail, learn and grow. If you want to find out if they've got what it takes, give them the space to make some mistakes. You can and should place safeguards, thresholds and limits on their decisions, to protect others, but the general trend should be one of increasing responsibility and trust.

Why? Because trusting someone tells them you respect them, which earns their respect and trust in return. In short, trust begets loyalty. As we learned from Paul Zak, when we show we really trust someone, it triggers the release of Oxytocin, which causes them to feel warm toward us and to trust us more.

Feeling empowered comes from feeling totally trusted. Those you lead, are more likely to be loyal – when you're not in the room – if they feel trusted. So, believe the best of them.

By way of contrast, four things diminish loyalty and drive people away from leaders:

1. Being micromanaged.

2. Being ordered to do something.

3. Critical remarks or hurtful humour.

4. Being made to look or feel incompetent.

These deplete loyalty because they all convey that you don't really trust someone, care about them or respect them.

"I feel hope"

Churchill is quoted as saying, *"I see no reason to be anything other than an optimist."*

In whatever capacity you lead, the people around you need to know you feel hopeful about the future. Hope energises others. And when you radiate enthusiasm, energy and passion, it's attractive to followers, as we discovered in the "Hope" chapter previously.

"I feel heard"

James 1:19 says, *"Be quick to listen, slow to speak, slow to anger."* That's very good advice. We should listen our way through a conflict or complaint, we can't just talk at people when they're angry. You cannot talk someone into feeling differently.

Often people just need to talk and to feel "heard." Let them vent their emotion. Sit quietly and absorb it; don't interrupt. Don't jump to defend yourself or attempt to set them right. Really listening to someone is the ultimate sign of respect: seeking to genuinely empathise and validate another person's feelings, thoughts and perspective.

In short, being a leader means people listen to you. But only if you listen to them first. Leadership is about respecting those who follow you, caring about them and really "hearing" them. It's the opposite of "bossing" people around and "telling" them what to do, giving the impression that you think you're the smartest person in the room with all the right answers. It's OK to ask for alternative opinions and invite different ideas; to seek out more pieces of the puzzle. By asking open questions (that cannot be answered with a "yes" or "no") you can draw suggestions and solutions out of your team rather than impressing your own.

No one enjoys being told when they've got it wrong but being a leader means being open to challenge. No one is perfect. Everyone makes mistakes. And we all have blind spots. Don't assume you know everything about a given problem. Don't guess at someone's motives or feelings. Make it your aim to keep getting a little better every day, by listening more than you speak. Always ask a question and remain quiet before you offer your own opinion. The best leaders I know are usually the last to speak in a meeting or group setting, especially when they have the final say. They wait, they listen, they show empathy, then they probe the problem and ask smart questions that draw out as many different options as possible.

Avoid being that clichéd caricature of a "boss" who has all of the power, and so assumes they know all the right answers. All of us are smarter than any of us. Steve Jobs of Apple famously used to say, "It doesn't make sense to hire smart people and tell them what to do; we hire smart people so they can tell *us* what to do."

"I feel held"

> *"Look, Hollom, it's leadership they want. Strength. Find that within yourself and you'll earn their respect."*
> **Captain Jack,** *Master and Commander*

The Capitulation-Domination Pendulum highlights the temptation to be too domineering and harsh – and then – too pacifying and indecisive.

The secret is to stay calm, confident and composed; to be strong for those you lead. And then to ask questions that allow people to discover and consider the likely consequences of different courses of action. You might call these "conse-questions." This approach enables those you lead to "feel held," not physically but emotionally. A strong and steady response will help to *contain* their fears, and then "conse-questions" *reframe* the challenge, allowing your team member to resolve their own problem.

To make it easy to remember, here's a tried and tested three-line framework you can follow:

1. **Assume the best (trust)**

2. **Hear the struggles (contain)**

3. **Ask conse-questions (reframe)**

Firstly, **assume the best** – which conveys *trust.*

Always expect the best of others' motives, behaviour and performance. People grow into your expectations of them, whether good or bad. So, speak well "to" and "of" people you lead. Show them you have high expectations of them and, time after time, they'll rise to meet your high standards and expectations.

Second, **make time to hear their struggles** – *contain* their fears.

Be a kind listener. Make time for those you lead. Take an interest in what's going on in their life. Remember their name, remember the personal details that matter. People follow leaders who care about them and listen to them. We view others based on how they make us feel. Don't just say that you're listening but show that you're listening by repeating back the salient points. This will help them "feel heard." Validating their viewpoint and understanding why they're upset, anxious or angry.

Don't jump in to solve their problem or to give an example of when you faced something similar. Listening attentively is an act of kindness.

This will almost always result in them feeling calmer and relieved to have had the chance to articulate their feelings. You may even notice them visibly relax in their chair.

They won't need or want a solution at this point, they just need to know you care; that you've heard and understood.

Thirdly, finally, **ask conse-questions** – *reframe* possible consequences as questions.

Be a calm questioner. Highlight the probable consequences of different courses of action, by asking questions that lead them to consider the effects and repercussions of various options they could choose.

Keep in mind the challenge: "Help me do it alone."

Don't tell them what to do, *ask them what it will do*. Let someone choose their own path, aiding them with conse-questions.

The person asking questions is the one in control of the conversation ultimately. So, you will have more power to influence and guide them than you may realise. Use this power gently and wisely. Your approach should leave them feeling stronger, more competent and more capable, as they come to their own conclusions and discover their own way forward.

Some useful questions to help them reframe reasons and ramifications are:

Have you considered...?

Have you thought about...?

What do you think will happen if...?

What impact do you think that might have had on...?

What do you think about the possibility that...?

What effect do you think that would have on...?

Will that option bring you closer to what you want?

What might achieve what you're looking for here?

Is there any other way it could be handled?

What are the different options you could try?

If you do need to lead someone to a specific solution, then "let's" can be a useful word. It lands more softly on the ear and on the heart, than "you need to."

Softer still is, "Shall we...?"

"Shall we" is a kinder, gentler way to set out a solution while leaving the person's dignity intact. It feels more like a deliberation between two equal partners. For instance, "All things considered, on this occasion shall we..."

If you're writing a difficult email or message, another tool you can use is the "best friend" test. Simply re-read what you've written and ask:

1. Would I write like this to my best friend?

2. Does this feel friendly or antagonistic?

3. Am I assuming the best of the other person here?

How to Challenge Behaviour

What about when rules are broken and behaviour must be called out and challenged more overtly?

There are some occasions when a direct challenge or even a reprimand may be necessary. Even in these times, it should be delivered with respect, humility and compassion. This team member should get a sense that you're acting out of care for them as well as concern for others.

When you do have to call out poor behaviour or under-performance, choose your words very carefully and do it face to face, not on email and not in front of other people.

Always start with "I" not with "you," for example "I felt" not "you caused."

Some softer phrases that can be useful when challenging someone are:

"I didn't appreciate it when..."

"I was surprised that..."

"I felt disappointed that..."

It can help to talk about the *effect* that the person's behaviour or decisions had on other team members, such as, "What effect do you think that had on X?"

Open the conversation up so they have a chance to share their side of the story and to feel heard. Then reaffirm your conclusions and decision:

"The bottom-line is... [the outcome of their behaviour on others] so [the resulting action]."

In these rare moments, you always pay a price. It will take time to build trust again and for the person to regain their confidence.

If someone categorically can't or won't agree with your dream destination, it's better that they leave and pursue a different one. If they stay, others in your team will become demoralised by this doubt and negativity.

In sum, trust others by believing the best of them, contain their feelings through calm, caring listening, then reframe the challenge, by asking open questions that highlight possible outcomes that may result from different responses.

Those you lead need to feel four things: to feel trusted, to feel hope, to feel heard, and to feel held, without feeling forced or coerced.

Frequent Flyer

- When your dream starts to soar, passengers start to complain. Avoid:
    - Self-pity
    - The Capitulation-Domination Pendulum

- The people you lead will need you to be strong and positive *for them*.

- Team members have four primary needs:
    - To FEEL TRUSTED (empower with high trust)
    - To FEEL HOPE (expect the best)
    - To FEEL HEARD (be a caring listener)
    - To FEEL HELD (be a calm questioner)

- A practical and proven method:
    - Assume the best (trust)
    - Hear the struggles (contain)
    - Ask conse-questions (reframe)

- Don't tell them what to do; ask them what it will do.

- Use the "best friend" test for contentious emails.

"The fool tells me his reason; the wise person persuades me with my own."
Aristotle

PART 3

"YAW"

LEADING FOR LONGEVITY

Money and other material assets are passed on to others when you pass away, but your reputation lives on as your legacy long after you've died.

Chapter 7
ELEVATORS:
HUMILITY & HONESTY
How your attitude sets your altitude

*"A good name is more desirable than great riches;
to be esteemed is better than silver or gold."*
Proverbs 22:1

If you ask a child to draw a castle, it will usually look like Rochester Castle in southeast England.

Built on a hilltop from hard grey limestone, this imposing Norman stronghold stands over a hundred feet from the ground. It has narrow arrow-slit windows positioned around its twelve feet thick walls, which are adorned with square turrets on the four corners. Each turret is crowned with crenelations affording lookouts a three hundred and sixty degree view to spot hostile forces from many miles away. Finally, the formidable structure is encircled on three sides by the river Medway, which acts as a natural moat and barrier. In fact, the castle was built just shy of one thousand years ago, to help guard a crossing point on the river; a natural barrier to marching armies strategically situated between London and mainland France.

For two hundred years, Rochester Castle did its job, standing strong as a seemingly impenetrable fortress, protecting the garrison within.

This all changed in 1215 AD, when King John marched on Rochester with an army to reassert his right to reign supreme over all of England.

Back in June of that year, the rich landowners who helped the King rule, had joined forces to compel the Monarch to relinquish some of his power. They demanded legal protection from unjust taxes and unfair treatment, such as being thrown in prison at the whim of the King. When King John placed his royal seal on a set of promises, he reluctantly conceded that The Crown would no longer be above the law of the land. In return, the barons agreed some concessions, such as handing Rochester Castle over to the Crown. This signed contract, curtailing the King's power, became known as *Magna Carta*, or *"Great Charter of Freedoms"* in the Latin of the day.

The ink had barely dried on this Royal charter of rights when the barons took up residence in Rochester Castle as an insurance policy, defiantly breaching their promise in the agreement. Occupying Rochester Castle was a fresh act of rebellion and it was the last straw for John. The King decided he wouldn't stand for this humiliation or any further restrictions on his power.

On 13 October, the King marched his army to Rochester, storming the bridge, invading the city and besieging the barons held up in the castle. The nobles retreated to the safety of the trusty tower with plenty of provisions, confident that the stronghold had already withstood two centuries of punishing attacks.

One year earlier, the King failed to reconquer his empire in France, and he didn't want to go down in history as a failure. John brought the full military might of his Royal war machine to bear, bombarding his own castle with the tanks and missiles of the mediaeval age. Day after day, night after night, for almost two months, trebuchet siege engines battered the walls with huge rocks that smashed chunks out of thick defences, but still the castle stood firm.

This is when King John deployed his most decisive tactical weapon.

Ultimately, it wasn't deadly crossbow bolts or devastating missiles that led to the barons' defeat. It was something far more clandestine. Just as later wars hinged on secretive breakthroughs, such as cracking Enigma, so this legendary siege ended with technological ingenuity; a highly secretive operation worthy of a mediaeval *Mission Impossible*.

While the barrage continued above ground, King John ordered military engineers to approach the castle undercover, literally. He instructed them to dig a tunnel known as a "sap," derived from the ancient French for a "spade." The royal engineers, or "sappers," burrowed beneath the castle's outer perimeter wall, reinforcing the passage with wooden support beams, until they finally reached the main castle structure and dug a void under the heavy stone walls.

To begin with, nothing happened.

But the Royal engineers had one last strategy up their sleeve. At the end of November, King John wrote to London commanding that forty fat pigs be brought to the battlefront. This was one hundred years before gunpowder came to England, and hog fat was used as a powerful explosive. The animals were placed below the castle walls, and a single torchbearer set fire to the wooden support beams, then ran for his life. As the timber burned into an inferno, the ground above it gave way and one corner of the stone castle collapsed into the sinkhole.

The nobles retreated to the top of the tower, but having sheltered inside for almost two months, their food supply had depleted and their morale dwindled away. The barons and their families were on the brink of starvation when they finally surrendered to the King in December 1215. Most were dismembered or put to death by the King.

The victory was short-lived. Just a year later, in 1216, King John died and there were rumours that the barons had arranged for him to be poisoned. Prince Louis then recaptured the famous castle after the barons appealed to the French for help defeating the Crown.

The question is, what can we learn from King John, his barons and this historic castle?

Eight hundred years later, the technique employed by the King is still a well-known term in common parlance:

To *"undermine"*

King John's legacy today is not his victory over the barons at Rochester Castle, rather he is remembered as incompetent, corrupt and cruel. In short, today we think of King John as a fool who was unfit to lead.

In fact, you've probably seen King John portrayed in a movie as a "bad king," without noticing the connection. In almost every retelling of "Robin Hood," King John features as a hapless, foolish and greedy ruler, hated by his subjects for unfair taxes and tyranny. He's usually compared with his heroic, brave brother King Richard the Lionheart who John succeeded. There is even a theory that the legendary myth of "Robin Hood" started life as one of the rebellious barons.

What will your legacy be?

It could be said that King John undermined his own legacy when he undermined his team and even his own castle.

Arguably, the whole tragic episode could have been averted if the barons had shown some *honesty* by keeping their word, and if the King had shown some *humility*, allowing the barons some concessions.

Had John chosen a more diplomatic and less aggressive response to the castle issue, perhaps he could have won the barons over and regained their trust. If he had, the chances are John would have remained as King of England – and indeed remained alive – with the willing support of his barons. His legacy would be very different, perhaps we would know him today as "John the Wise." It was within his power to win a reputation for showing mercy, wisdom, fairness and canny diplomacy. King John could have been the King Solomon of his age, with a celebrated reign of justice and peace.

Instead, John literally undermined the co-owners of his kingdom. He destroyed his own strategically located castle, cutting off his nose to spite his face. John's pride, rage and lust for power led to his downfall and secured his place in history and legend as a bad king.

But the barons are far from blameless. They were the King's "team," who had successfully won the rights and freedoms they craved. Despite this victory, their hubris and cynical mistrust led them to occupy the castle and break their side of the bargain. Their lack of honesty and integrity ultimately lit the fuse of their own demise. The nobility certainly didn't act in a noble way, and as a result, they lost everything and plunged their country into civil war. They forfeited their role in leading a peaceful and fair realm. As a result, the barons' legacy is to be remembered as being two-faced and weak; fickle promise-breakers, who snatched defeat from the jaws of victory.

The question is, what will your legacy be?

What figurative castle are you building? And who's the team at your side?

Are you, or they, behaving in any way that threatens to undermine your achievements and legacy?

This chapter is about two critical qualities you need to leave a lasting legacy you can feel proud of and be pleased with.

There are some key lessons to take from this historical tale, and your ability to learn and absorb these truths will determine what your legacy will be, and ultimately, how you'll be remembered by others.

The Reputation Rule

The Reputation Rule dictates that *everything you do builds your reputation, whether positive or negative.*

A good reputation has currency and value. It cannot be bought but must be earned. It could be said that "Reputation is Royalty," in terms of the true power and influence it affords.

But a good reputation is also fragile, it takes years to build but can be destroyed in seconds, due to bad judgement.

If you lose a good reputation, then everything you've built will be undermined and collapse in an instant. It will take years to rebuild it and restore people's trust and respect for you.

You can undermine your own skills and hard work, and forfeit your dreams, by acting dishonestly or pridefully. The great castle you've been building for months, years or even decades will come crashing down and you'll have nothing left to show for your efforts.

Humility and Honesty

Two "elevators" will keep you from descending when you're flying high and well on your way to your dream destination. They'll also prevent you from stalling and falling from the sky, if you get too high minded and proud:

- **Humility**, to guard against **pride, ego** and **foolish arrogance.**

- **Honesty,** to overcome the temptation of **dishonesty**, taking shortcuts to success, pleasure or prosperity.

Pride and dishonesty are dangerous pitfalls. Either one can send your reputation into a nosedive; tainting your idea or project. It's just a matter of time.

The sad thing is that you can take many other passengers down with you. Your followers, team and even your project's beneficiaries will be dragged down as well. If you fall, they fall and lose out too. The hurt, damage and harm is never restricted to the leader alone. Private moral failing or dishonesty will create ripple effects that you can't control or ever take back.

Once you're a leader, people are following but also copying you. You're setting the tone, the pace, the culture by what you say, but *more so* by what you do. You are being watched. How you live, how you speak to other people, how you treat those with less power or money than you. Leaders are role models. It's a package deal.

In short, your attitude and character will always determine your altitude as a leader; how high you rise and how much success you see in your endeavours.

Hubris Hurts You

As a leader and Someday dreamer, figuratively speaking you're creating your own castle.

You have a vision, a blueprint in your mind, to build something important that will last and stand the test of time; something solid and stable that will provide shelter or inspiration to other people for years to come.

But you risk undermining your own dream castle, if you let hubris, greed and pride get the better of you.

In the wise words of Jesus:

"Every kingdom divided against itself is brought to desolation; and every city or house divided against itself shall not stand." **Matthew 12:25**

When King John attacked his own city and undermined his own team, his kingdom began to crumble at the same moment as his castle. Likewise, when your team challenge you, question your actions or provoke you by making demands, don't allow your anger and ego to distract you from the real goal. Hubris only hurts you. In other words, you'll undermine your own legacy and ruin your own castle, if you do undermine your team or begin working against them. Instead, act in the pursuit of reconciliation, diplomacy and unity. After all, to err is human, but to forgive is divine.

So, don't backbite, scheme and seek revenge. Don't pour your finite energies into getting retribution. Just let things go. Overlook the offence. Find a way to get along with your co-builders and focus on something that matters much more: sharing the castle and working together on your shared dream.

Humility

> *"Do not think of yourself more highly than you ought, but rather think of yourself with sober judgement... We have different gifts... If your gift is to lead, do it diligently."* **Romans 12:3-8**

I like the word "diligently" here. It's from the Latin "diligere," which means "to love and take delight in." We should *take delight* in leading others and even aspire to *love* them, rather than lord it over people or use them to get what we want. Our aim should be to find "delight" in encouraging, inspiring, coaching, supporting and helping the people we lead and influence.

The truth is, being a leader means you're simply fulfilling *one role* in a team. Your function is to serve the team with your gifts. Leadership gifts are not any better or superior to any other gift that the team needs to succeed. No billionaire CEO can run their company alone, for instance. Remove the team and the leader is literally "useless," that's the bottom-line. It's an interdependent partnership, between the leader and the team, to serve others, whether beneficiaries or customers.

I always think of Jesus washing his disciples sweaty, dusty feet, to actively model humility and servant-heartedness. Unless you think you're wiser and more important than Jesus, don't take yourself too seriously. "Don't think of yourself more highly than you ought."

Instead, believe in yourself, so others can too, but don't boast or wave your credentials in the face of others. Those who are forever telling people how gifted, rich and successful they are, usually appear insecure and arrogant at best. Some of the most inspiring leaders I've met are quick to ask subordinates when they lack the knowledge or expertise in a given area. They say things like, "Please can you help me understand this better?"

Likewise, don't put yourself down. And don't be your own worst critic. No one will treat you better than you treat yourself. Plus, being needy is creepy and counterproductive. No one benefits from you being embarrassed or reluctant to lead. If you don't believe in yourself, who else will? Don't look to your team to tell you what a helpful and inspiring leader you are and how much they need you.

Equally, don't ever feel anyone is above you. If you need to talk to someone, go and find them. Respect people, not titles. Put another way, arrogance is thinking you're above people, but confidence is knowing no one is above you.

Instead, be quietly confident, without thinking it's all about you and without thinking less of anyone else. Be kind to those who are sharing the workload with you. Never put another person down or underestimate their role. And don't belittle anyone, whether to their face or behind their back. Without other people with different skills and strengths than you, you won't get far in life.

On the other hand, don't tip the scale the other way and over-praise people in an attempt to get what you want. Disingenuous flattery makes it hard for people to respect you.

Honesty = Integrity

"Be people of integrity. No deceit. If you don't have integrity at the end of your life, you don't have much."
Don Stephens, *founder of Mercy Ships*

Dishonesty can be defined as, "a purposeful personal or business moral failing or an intentional lapse in integrity."

"Integrity" comes from the word "integer," which means "whole." To have integrity is to bring the same whole person to each sphere of your life – your private life, your professional life, your friendships and your public appearances. This doesn't mean telling everyone everything about you; it means that you're never deceiving anyone, you're only ever revealing something from the same whole version of you. You aren't inventing or hiding anything. Your whole life needs to be consistent with what you say and what you ask of others.

This means that you cannot separate out personal integrity at home and when socialising from professional integrity at work or in your career circles. You are one person and your character encompasses every aspect of your "whole" life.

Integrity is more valuable than money.

Money and other material assets are passed on to others when you pass away, but your reputation lives on as your legacy long after you've died. Integrity is therefore the most priceless quality you can possess during your lifetime. Your reputation will be your most precious asset; so invest well while you still can.

Think of any famous person from history: their lasting reputation is first and foremost a result of their character and moral choices. From world leaders to sports stars, business entrepreneurs to church leaders – after you're gone, what remains is the kind of person you were, far more so than the accomplishments you achieved or the wealth you amassed. A good name is worth protecting.

Most of the time, this won't be too difficult to stay true to your values and practice what you preach. But on occasions you'll be tempted to take a shortcut or live in a way that's inconsistent with your beliefs or the culture of your community or organisation. When you feel low or misunderstood, or when you can see a quick win that will benefit others, you may feel a pull to justify a behaviour or decision that falls short of your usual standard and the standard you ask of others around you. If you hear your own inner monologue working hard to find a loophole, that should always be a red flag. You may find yourself coming back to internal justifications that sound like this:

"No one will find out, and I'll only do it once."

"It's okay because it will help everyone get closer to our destination."

"I'm tired. I've been working so hard to serve others, I deserve this."

And the old favourite:

"I know I say not to do this to my team, but I'm the leader, so it's different for me. I'm facing different pressures and challenges they'll never understand."

If you find phrases like these creeping into your consciousness, question and kill them. Call them out as lies and recognise them as the slippery slope into dishonesty that can destroy your biggest asset – your reputation.

All you have in this world, when all is said and done, is your good reputation.

You can't be one person on a platform and a different one backstage. You can't be two people at once. What's more, the words we say in secret have a habit of finding their way back to the person they were spoken about.

Now more than ever, in an age of CCTV, mobile phones, social media, location tracking, e-banking and internet history – your digital footprint will always leave a trail back to the truth. Few secrets remain so forever and those that do will still affect the decisions you make. Repressed guilt will impact your sleep and mental health and the people you are closest with can always tell when you're hiding something. Once your mistake or misjudgement is found out it will then erode the trust and loyalty you depend upon to lead your followers somewhere better.

What we say and who we are, both have to be in sync. Being loyal to your own values, means being true to ourselves every day. As Simon Sinek puts it: "Values are verbs, not nouns. We have to enact our values in how we show up every day."

Focus on the qualities that qualify you to lead and not on your title or past achievements.

A leader isn't the person with the biggest pay packet or the most impressive CV. A leader is someone who puts in more hours, studies harder and cares enough to do things "by the book."

Do you ever find yourself watching a family tree programme on TV, where celebrities find out about their ancestors and genealogy? What they discover about their forebears can leave them feeling a huge sense of pride and admiration, or sometimes deep shame, sadness and disappointment.

Your children, grandchildren and great grandchildren will likely learn what you tried so hard to keep hidden, even if you strain to conceal things during your lifetime. If you don't have any biological descendants, you will certainly have followers connected to your dream or a community that may lose faith and wander away from everything you worked to build if they discover one day that you weren't who you purported to be.

When a respected and revered leader falls from grace, so to speak, the collateral damage extends far beyond their family and dependents. It sends out seismic shockwaves that hurt everyone connected to the dream, team or project. You can do damage without ever meaning to, simply by believing "no one but me can get hurt by this." Your name will come to embody something after you're gone, whether distinction, disgrace or some middle ground in between.

Do you want to be remembered as a byword for "such a shame" or "they-could-have-been"? Along with your reputation, the values you toiled to instil in others can unravel in an instant. When you fail, so does your legacy and your life's work. The product of all your labour goes from solid obsidian to shattered oblivion in the blink of an eye. People drift away damaged, demoralised and disappointed. What's more, they will often become disillusioned and hesitant to put their trust in another leader like you or to hope for a dream destination again in future.

When you do fall down, personally or through a questionable leadership decision, the best thing you can do for yourself and other people is to get straight back up. The longer you're down, the more time you waste. Wallowing in self-pity is an indulgence you can't afford.

You may be down, but you're not out. If you're still breathing, then you're not beaten. So, get up and keep going. Tomorrow is a new day. You'll only reach your destination if you get back up and keep moving towards it.

As a Christian, I believe no one can ever truly fall from grace, in a literal sense. God can and will always forgive someone if they're truly sorry and seeking to turn-around and do life differently. We all mess up and make mistakes, so perpetual perfection is not required for any leader. What is required is an ongoing pursuit of transparency, honesty and personal integrity. Every leader is in a daily battle against hypocrisy and temptation. The greatest temptations are to compromise, conceal or cover up dubious decisions, during our highest highs or lowest lows. Leaders are most vulnerable immediately after they achieve mountain top acclaim, praise and success, when they begin to believe they're special or superior. The person who feels exceptional can believe they should be an exception to the rules that apply to other people.

In stark contrast, in moments of extreme frustration, failure, fatigue or fear, a leader can be tempted to "take a gamble" to "win at all costs," especially if they see someone else enjoying the spoils of success after cutting corners and getting away with it. This amounts to little more than an adult version of the toddler's cry, "It's not fair!" That's when leaders often do something impulsive, selfish and foolish with no regard for the consequences.

Long after you're dead and gone, your legacy will be based on who you were, not what you did. Whether you pushed others down to pull yourself up. How you used what you were given. And whether you invested your time and talents to improve the lives of others. Your reputation will determine how you are perceived in perpetuity:

Have you ever heard something akin to, "They have no credibility left after what they did"?

This is not a statement about the person's abilities or track record – it's about their actions **undermining** their dreams and their legacy.

Even during your lifetime, your capacity to affect change and your capability to lead others with influence, will never grow beyond the level of your character.

It's integrity that affords you credibility, here and now; without which you cannot exert influence. In fact, the very dictionary definition of "credible" is to be: *"worthy of belief and capable of being believed."*

You simply cannot be a credible leader, unless you are trustworthy and quite literally, "worthy of people's trust."

That's why you need to practise what you preach, so your followers will be able to trust you and believe what you tell them. They'll be able to respect you and so follow you because you have credibility.

"Liars, when they speak the truth, aren't believed."
Aristotle

You undermine your own success and achievements with dishonest decisions and unkind words. Double-talk or duplicitous backstabbing tells people that you can't be trusted. As the wise African Proverb expresses, *"He who speaks to you about others, speaks to others about you."*

"Seeing is different to being told" ~ African proverb

How you live and what you do, resounds decibels louder than anything you say. You lead by what you model far more than what you speak, regardless of whether you teach, preach, train, coach or consult. Pastor Celia Apeagyei-Collins says it best, *"Leaders model then followers mimic."*

In other words, your conduct as a leader is what you'll construct in your followers.

We can often think, when we don't like a behaviour or culture we see, that telling someone straight is the most effective way to bring about the change. That's not how human beings operate. People are far more likely to watch how their leader speaks, acts and responds, and then they will gauge the merits of that leader's life. If followers see something they like, they'll aim to mimic and emulate it. That's why personal integrity and honesty are so important for every leader. You must live as you lead.

This is where pride and ego can trip leaders up. They see people mimicking them, and they begin to believe they're someone very special.

Being a successful leader certainly does not exempt you from adhering to the values and behaviours you expect from others, nor does it elevate you above your team members.

"Character may almost be called the most effective means of persuasion."
Aristotle

Humility and Honesty are elevators. They'll help you rise as a leader by enabling others to trust you, respect you and follow you, even into stormy skies and choppy waters.

So, stay humble and be the same honest and authentic person no matter who you are with. Be worthy of those who are watching you and following you. Then you will become that rare thing, a greatly respected and trustworthy leader with noble character. A leader who holds to the highest moral standards and ethical principles. Someone people feel safe to believe and trust. Someone they can respect, even if they disagree with a decision.

Unless you lead and live in an honest way with honest words and deeds, people will quickly feel you're not safe to lead them and they'll walk away from you. But when you model it, they'll follow it. As the saying goes, "you can't be what you can't see."

Frequent Flyer

- Hubris Hurts You: You can undermine the figurative castle you're trying to build.

- Don't undermine your team: "A kingdom divided against itself... shall not stand."

- The Reputation Rule: Everything you do builds your reputation.

- Reputation is Royalty: A good reputation has currency and value. It's earned over a long time. It's also fragile; it can be destroyed in seconds.

- You cannot separate personal integrity from professional integrity; your character encompasses your whole life.

- When a respected leader falls, the shockwaves hurt everyone connected to their dream.

- Your capacity to affect change will never grow beyond your character.

- Your integrity affords you credibility, without which you cannot exert influence.

- Your conduct as a leader is what you'll construct in your followers: When you model it, they will follow it.

- Humility and Honesty are elevators; these character traits will determine your *altitude* as a leader.

"Men/Women acquire a particular quality by constantly acting in a particular way."
Aristotle

There can be no lasting success without succession. We only truly succeed when we are succeeded.

Chapter 8
LANDING GEAR: HANDOVER
How to land well

"I don't need to be the best."

These are the words of Chris Martin, the lead singer of Coldplay. This band can fill stadiums and they've sold over one hundred million records worldwide.

I heard him talking to another gifted and hard-working artist who, Chris admits, is a much better musician than him. Yet Chris Martin wasn't threatened. In fact, he seemed to enjoy learning and listening to the genius of another composer and performer. He even compared his friend to Mozart, tears welling in his eyes; a virtuoso who was head and shoulders above his peers.

Chris Martin is at the top of his game. He's performed to hundreds of thousands of people, won acclaim and awards, and written some of the world's most memorable and popular songs, and yet, he's still able to say publicly, "*It's okay. I don't need to be the best.*"

Chris Martin isn't defined by his music. He's not jealous of others, or at least, he strives not to be. And he's not trying to compete; to beat other bands and win at all costs. Chris simply wants to make good music and help make the world a better and fairer place for everyone. And so, he cheers his friend on, even inviting Jacob Collier to help him arrange the chords and harmonies for an album so Chris can learn from a better musician and other renowned music producers.

We all need to get to that place: where we can create things and make things, without these creations becoming the root of our identity.

The lesson here?

You are not the best thing you've ever made.

You are not the worst thing you've ever done.

You are not what you create.

What you make is not what gives you value.

The people in your field of work and the entities in your sphere of expertise, may be competitors but they're certainly not your enemies.

No. The enemy is hopelessness. The enemy is injustice and suffering.

Our common enemy is poverty. And disease. And hatred.

We work together to defeat these dangerous foes.

So, relax and let go. Let others do well or even better than you. And cheer them on, with a smile, not through gritted teeth.

Go on the journey together. Spur one another on. Learn together.

Make this your ultimate goal: to become the kind of giant that lifts other people up, to stand on your shoulders.

This chapter is about this generous, courageous and counter-cultural mindset:

Letting others take YOUR vision to new places and further than you ever could.

Becoming a launch pad for their dreams and handing over yours to the next generation.

Landing is Painful

When you're inventing the first plane with an engine, capable of staying airborne and climbing high in the sky, you can't overlook one crucial fact: You'll have to learn how to land.

Orville Wright had no choice in this respect. He and his brother invented the first heavier than air aircraft with an onboard propulsion system, so they also had to come up with a safe way to slow down, descend and get back on the ground in one piece. One without the other, lift off without landing, would not make for a very long career as the first pilots of a powered plane.

Today's modern jet airliners land with clever onboard computers, but the steps are the same as for Wright's flying machine: descend and slow down, stop safely and walk away.

When we travel in a jet aircraft, the pilots create reverse thrust on the engines to slow down, and they raise the spoilers on the wings, to create drag to descend. As they approach the runway, they lower the landing gear and dim the lights in the cabin, in case passengers have to exit the plane quickly in the dark. Landing requires absolute focus, careful consideration of the environment and conditions and an "adjustment" period for those disembarking.

Likewise, every successful leader has to know how to land their dream. Put simply, this means learning to let go and being willing to walk away. All of the disciplined HABITS and courageous HEART you developed to get your vision to lift off the ground and fly high, must be summoned to land the dream, figuratively switching these leadership qualities into Reverse-Mode, like the giant jet engines on modern planes. As we step back, and even step away, others can then step forward and step up to take our place.

In short, there can be no lasting success without succession. Since we only truly succeed when we are succeeded. That's why the sub-title of this book is supposed to make you look twice. You expect to read the word "succeed," but instead you notice the less common term, "*secede*". This ancient word, "secede," comes from the Latin "*secedere*," meaning "*to withdraw, yield completely, go apart from.*" The Latin "*cedere*," is also the root of the word "*succeed*," meaning to "follow after" or "achieve a desired aim" — and of the word "*concede,*" meaning "to yield or surrender."

We only truly *succeed* in achieving our goal when we *secede* from it, *conceding* our dream to others, by passing the baton over to new dreamers and leaders, who will run with it and take it further than we ever could. To put it another way: your arrival at the ultimate destination of succession is the definition of lasting and bona fide success.

There can be no Lasting Success Without a Successor

Just look at the life and work of a leader you admire: the secret of their success will be succession. Every great and truly enduring leader learns how to hand over and raise up other leaders.

If you observe companies, charities or churches that are led by one gifted and hugely charismatic and capable founder, when they move on, retire or die, "their" movement or community can quickly stall and stagnate or even just stop altogether. These organisations lose their way, they forget their values and forsake their core purpose. The truth is that a little money in the bank, a good helping of brand loyalty and residual cultural momentum may carry the enterprise a little longer and a little further, but eventually without the leader keeping the thing on course and providing inspiration and direction, it can all grind to a halt.

Where emerging leaders haven't been identified, encouraged, trained, supported, coached and empowered to succeed, even the greatest organisations crumble and their followers will flounder or their customers will drift away. The causes they met then wait for a new leader who understands the nine Plane Parable traits.

Almost anyone can grow in people skills over time and most do. Many people live decent and kind lives a lot of the time. And some dreamers will develop the habits they need to succeed in new undertakings. Yet few leaders learn how to hand over.

The most rewarding feeling you can experience as a leader is seeing those who follow you, go beyond and further than you. That shouldn't fill you with dread or frustration, it should fill you with peace and a deep sense of satisfaction, because your mantras, your ideas, your values and ways of working will live on, long after you're gone. You have truly created something that will last and make a multi-generational difference.

This simple fact is the secret that so many leaders miss out on. Even leaders who enjoy recruiting, building and empowering teams and who find this rewarding, can fail to grasp the final and full secret of success. To succeed you need to *cede*; to give up power, to yield hard-won territory, to allow someone else to have their turn and chance to lift off and soar. There can be no lasting or meaningful success without succession of some nature.

This is why knowing your motives is so important, you can loosen your grip on what you've taken a leading role in creating, without losing your sense of self-worth and identity. Your "why" should outlast and outlive every expression of your calling and purpose. You are not what you create, and you are not what you do. You can be whole without clinging to what you contribute, your accolades and your position of influence.

The most painful "H"

Without a doubt, the hardest "H" of the nine needs, is "Handover."

After all, why should you let someone else climb up on your back to reach the fruit of a tree that you planted and lovingly nurtured.

Because you'll die someday. To be blunt.

If you never give your dream away, your dream will die too. If you don't give away your skills, your learning, your ideas and your incredible capacity to bring about a positive change in the world, then all these things will fade with your name and memory. The same goes for your money. You can't take it with you, but it can work and do good after you're gone.

If you want to guarantee long-term success and leave a lasting legacy, then work for the success of the leaders who are following you. This is how you lead for *longevity*.

Barack Obama says, "You should be predisposed to other people's power. How can I make the people around me do great things? Give them the tools. Get rid of the barriers. Help coach them. Organise them."

Yes, letting go is hard. Let go anyway.

One of my favourite musicals is Hamilton.

Towards the end of the performance, you watch George Washington rescind his power freely and under no obligation to do so. He had literally fought wars as a general and helped found a country against all the odds of British military might. After serving for two terms as the first-ever President of the United States he relinquished power and stepped down.

The whimsical King George III of Great Britain sings a very poignant lyric:

"They say, George Washington's yielding his power and stepping away. Is that true?

I wasn't aware that was something a person could do. I'm perplexed."

So, why did Washington give up his power? Because he feared if he were to die while in office, Americans would think of the presidency as a lifetime appointment.

Great Britain was a monarchy. The Ruler ruled for life. George Washington knew the secret to success in the long-haul is succession; to create something that can be handed from generation to generation, and doesn't depend on one fallible founder or their personal fame, powerbase or following.

This is actually how academia works, one researcher works on a prediction or a "thesis," building on the knowledge of generations who have gone before them, then another person will build on top of that and another on top of that. A profound discovery published in a PhD will one day be a quick chapter in a school textbook. $E = mc^2$ is something we can all recite, whereas once it only occurred to one dreamer: Albert Einstein.

Those who do great things in life often say in speeches, "I stood on the shoulders of giants."

Now, you can be a small leader, whose idea turns to dust when they do. In that case, your work will only carry on until the momentum of your movement and the voice of your convictions vanishes, like a morning mist. Or you can be a giant of a leader. You can give it all away and leave a lasting legacy.

You can teach others to fish in the pools you dug. You can coach the next *you*, when you spot someone with potential in your team. You can even write a book, record a podcast or make videos, sharing with a wider audience your ideas, values and beliefs and tools and tips for making them work.

Long-haul leaders know the secret to success is succession.

Gripping onto a leadership position, a place of influence or a former glory for as long as possible is futile and not a good look.

Perhaps you're a younger leader? That just means you need to start getting into the habit of letting go and trying something new while you have less to lose. As you get older it gets increasingly harder to leave a high perch and hop down to try a new endeavour. When you have a mortgage, a steady job, and kids to provide for, starting over will feel more of a risk and challenge.

The beauty of succession is that we get to stand on the shoulders of others and each time we do we're able to see a little further than they did. To the next horizon and dream destination.

It's a selfless way to lead because you know other people will go places you couldn't. Whether that's your team, your children or your grandchildren. It's okay that they start where you finished — that's how it's supposed to work. Rest assured, they'll have their own colossal mountains to scale, their own internal demons to fight and their own antagonists and haters to overcome. Life is hard enough and you get to give them a head start.

Everyone wins when they use that advantage to do something that enriches other people's lives.

> *"The greatest leader is not necessarily the one who does the greatest things.*
> *They are the one who gets the people to do the greatest things."*
> **President Ronald Reagan**

How to Handover

There are four stages for raising up leaders you can handover to:

1. **Tell**

2. **Sell**

3. **Empower**

4. **Delegate** and **Celebrate**

At the start, your dream will have a honeymoon period, where you just have to **TELL** others your vision. In this phase, people are naturally drawn to you because of the picture you paint of a desirable future destination. That's when you "form" your team of helpers or followers.

We then talked about what happens when a team hits the "storming" stage. You can't miss it. The conflicts, arguments and complaints will come thick and fast. And the way ahead suddenly seems almost foggy, as stress and indecision cloud your judgement, and you lose sight of your goal for a moment. When real life kicks in, trouble and setbacks emerge, as a leader you must **SELL** the dream, using stories that remind people where they're going and why it's important; stories which give people hope and quench their doubts and fears.

Thirdly, your team begins to "norm." As a leader you can (and must) step back a bit. Your role here is to simply **EMPOWER** the team, individually and collectively, helping them feel "held," and using careful "Conse-questions" to allow team members to see the possible consequences of various options in order to make good decisions on their own. Remember the unspoken cry, "Help me do it alone!"

Finally, the part most leaders miss or are too proud to carry out – when the team is performing without you, you have to let go and throw everything you have at slowing down and stopping (to allow others to "perform" and you yourself to step back out of the limelight). This is where the leader role is to **DELEGATE and CELEBRATE**; to allow the team and the rising stars beneath you to shine and take on more and more of the decisions and responsibilities. You move from being a coach, calling the plays at the side of the field, to the chair-person in the stands. You're making far fewer decisions but having to get the really big calls right and operating at a higher level, where you can see the whole field and even the fans in the stands (or the market) to stretch the metaphor.

It's not fun to slow down and to step up. And many leaders struggle. They feed off the adrenaline and the buzz of the factory-floor, when really they're needed in the boardroom, where they can be more level-headed and objective. What you lose in this phase, where the team is performing on its own, is some of the fun of being "one of the team," but you gain perspective and headspace that will benefit those you lead. What the team needs from you in this moment is for you to be unclouded by the crisis and complexities of the day-to-day running of things and so able to bring a fresh perspective and cool head. They need you to be free to look further ahead, once again. They need you to glimpse the new destination and begin plotting the course. It may spoil your fun, but it's what the team and the vision need in this moment.

This is when succession planning kicks in, handing over the reins to someone fresh and even more skilled than you in some areas. The truth is that entrepreneurs and founders are seldom experts in one field; they're able to flex and adapt to different markets and fields and have the vision, energy and communication skills to launch multiple projects, one after the other.

"It's only as we develop other people that we permanently succeed."
Harvey Firestone

People will remember the end of your "flight" more than how you started.

Finishing well matters more than your novice beginning.

The true mark of a great leader and dreamer is whether they can hand over their dream and pass the baton to a new generation. Few leaders manage to scale this final hurdle and pass this test, which can lead to leaving a lasting legacy.

The truth is that succession and handover is the natural and most profound aspect of arriving at a dream destination. It's actually freeing, although painful to begin with.

If your team is up and running and you're exhausting yourself trying to keep up and get out in front of them all the time, perhaps you need to stop and just let them go. Maybe, your season is one of rest and refuelling.

The beautiful truth is that when you stop, that's when the next idea comes. That's when the new destination flickers on your radar screen. And that's when you realise the people you've let run with your old vision are still running with it and they'll take it higher and further than you ever could.

The end of the summer is when you cut roses right back. They need to use all their energy, in the colder months, to stop producing pretty flowers and do the unseen work of driving down roots to take in nutrients from the soil. Low and behold, in the spring season, stunning new roses appear – brighter, more fragrant and more vibrant than before. It looks like nothing's happening, but the period without flowers and fruit is often a plant's most important season.

Likewise, stopping and handing over is a natural season and process. It gives you time to rest, reflect and envisage a new dream destination. With handover comes revitalisation, space and freedom to think and dream afresh.

If you land well, and display the character and strength to hand over, then you have attained the accolade of being a long-haul leader: someone who leads for longevity by leaving a lasting legacy in the lives of others. That is true success.

Frequent Flyer

- What you do, is not what gives you value.

- Don't compete. Work alongside others to defeat a common enemy: injustice.

- We only truly succeed when we're succeeded.

- Your arrival at the destination of succession is the definition of success.

- If you never give away your dream, you will never create lasting change in the world.

- Finishing well matters more than how you started. People remember the end more clearly.

- With handover comes revitalisation, space and freedom, to think and dream afresh.

- Become a long-haul leader: someone who leads for longevity by leaving a legacy.

"Well begun is half done."
Aristotle

THE PLANE PARABLE

When you share the problem with other people who come from different backgrounds, you're able to expand your brain power into a supercomputer.

Chapter 9
Prologue: The beginning?

We've reached our destination: the end of the book. So, where are you on your journey? Perhaps, you're just at the beginning?

On the Runway

If you've been waiting to finish the book before you take your first steps in the real world, then now is the time. Don't wait as doubt will creep in. Act now. Set a date, tell a friend or write your Purpose Statement. Make some positive and intentional move in the direction of your dream destination. Whatever you decide, do something. Start somewhere. You need to start before you feel ready.

And don't stay in the planning and note-writing phase too long. You don't need to have all the answers before you begin, or even all the funds. You'll learn as you go and hone your ideas, through trial and error. The sooner you start, the more time you'll have to get better at finding your way, raising money and recruiting people.

The only way to steer a boat is to take it out in open water. A rudder is useless on dry land.

It's been said that people waste time in the same way every day. Don't wait for Someday to happen to you. Instead, make Someday today. Get going down that runway, gather some speed and pull up.

All Aboard!

There's an African proverb, "If you want to go fast, go alone, if you want to go far go together."

If you've started working towards your dream, perhaps you're ready to pitch your vision and build a team.

Building a team will always take your dream further, as they get to share in the achievement and make it their dream too.

Recruitment is key to making dreams happen. It's essential that you pick good people. Ultimately, what you're looking for is "Honesty," "Humility" and "Heart" as well as someone who shares your vision for the same dream destination.

When you're looking for team members, don't only choose people who are like you. Surround yourself with people who think differently and who may know more than you about their area of expertise.

Most of us like being with and leading people who are "like us," but this makes for weak teams. What you need is diversity, in terms of ethnicity, background, experience, gender, strengths and thinking style. Think of your team as an extension of your own mind. You can process a certain amount of data and your own brain will come up with one or two solutions. But when you share the problem with other people who come from different backgrounds, who have different life experiences, read different books and have different aptitudes to you, you're able to expand your brain power into a supercomputer. Don't think that a leader should sit in a little room, all alone, working everything out in isolation.

You don't just want people who will agree with you all the time. You need some alternative viewpoints. You also need people who will encourage and support you, people who will "have your back" and who are naturally optimistic.

Heading into the Storm

If you're in the middle of your "flight," and you have others onboard who are already working with you (or even relying on you) then now is not the time to quit.

You may be in the middle of a storm or experiencing some "turbulence." If so, now is the time to dig in and to revisit the Hope, Heard and Held chapters.

Ready for the Next Journey?

When a plane arrives at an airport, sometimes it stops to refuel and it certainly lets the passengers off, but it always gets back up in the air. Otherwise, rust sets in. A plane is designed to spend most of its life in the air, not on the ground.

Have you been resting and reflecting long enough?

Is this your time to get ready to take off again? Is it time to form the next team and cast another vision? Is it time to dream a new dream?

Never again will you truly start from scratch. You will be taking every lesson you learned from your last flight into your next venture. You now have more skills, strategies, networks, resources, real-life experience and, maybe, even funds. This all means, you can fly faster, further and higher. Not every leader masters long-haul leadership. But you will.

The pilot is ready.

The passengers are waiting.

You're cleared for take-off.

Where to now?

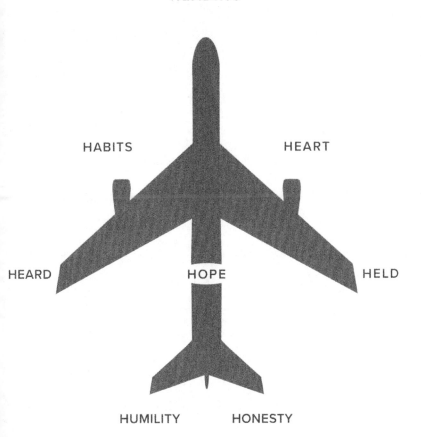

HEADING

HABITS   HEART

HEARD   HOPE   HELD

HUMILITY   HONESTY

HANDOVER

About the Author

Darren is an international author-speaker, broadcaster and advisor.

As a leaders' leader with twenty years' experience in the non-profit sector, his passion is telling stories that empower others to make a difference.

Darren has mobilised thousands of volunteers to help others and has led teams that have raised millions of pounds for charitable causes and community projects.

A trustee of *Young Emerging Leaders,* he also hosts the "Someday Arrival" podcast, to equip emerging leaders and encourage Someday dreamers.

Darren is married to Caroline and they live with their twin sons in the UK.

Printed in Great Britain
by Amazon

22336801R00116